Zoe

C000079448

SWEET DREAMS

By

Andrew J Turvill

Grosvenor House
Publishing Limited

The right of Andrew J Turvill to be identified as the author of this
work has been asserted in accordance with Section 78
of the Copyright, Designs and Patents Act 1988

The book cover is copyright to Andrew J Turvill

This book is published by
Grosvenor House Publishing Ltd
Link House
140 The Broadway, Tolworth, Surrey, KT6 7HT.
www.grosvenorhousepublishing.co.uk

A CIP record for this book
is available from the British Library

ISBN 978-1-83975-412-8

Twenty-five years and my life is still, trying to get up that great big hill of hope... for a destination.

Introduction

When I started this project many years ago, I did not know where it was going and how in-depth I wanted to go. I did not know if I could face up to some things I had been running from for a very long time. I found that confronting them head on made me stronger and I was no longer afraid of anything that I had endured. I came at it from a point of anguish and wanting to release everything I had held onto for so many years. Some people ask you what you're doing with your life, they judge you on where they think you should be – I've been guilty of the same, but I understood that I was doing it differently to others. Others different from me. There's no pattern. Everyone just does what they must, to enable them to get by. We should all know that we are not alone in this, it's the one thing that unifies us, that none of us really know what the hell we are doing.

From this point in time, I looked back at everything I have experienced, good and bad; I realized one thing, that what I was doing with my life, was healing. From a place of trauma that took me 25 years to overcome – a quarter of a century, that seems such a long time now. 25 years since it stopped anyway, and some things beginning, but I think back to who I was then at that time, in those moments when I was coping. Surviving. I respect that version of me for being so strong as to survive, because if I hadn't, then I wouldn't be here today. I look back and see some of the things that I did were not appropriate or deemed normal by most, but whatever I did, I did to survive in extreme circumstances. I was a normal child for most parts, but was dealing with huge burdens from influences out of mine and my family's control. Maybe I could have been a better version of myself today, but with all the influences of things that happened, who else could I be? I am doing my all to be the best version of myself. Some people will get a different version of me, but this is the real version of me. Some may have seen aspects and caught snippets, but this is everything that I am and have been.

The irony of the passing of time isn't lost on me and at times, I feel that I have wasted so much time – I have wasted my hours and seconds just doing nothing. I should see this as recovering, if you have a major operation you don't just move around really quickly. Mentally, this is the same. You take it day by day, step by step. I look back at myself, say 20 years ago, I was clearly a complete mess, but at that time I thought I had it so together. I'm dumbfounded by how no-one saw this. Then, myself and my sister were masters at hiding things, because we both had secrets that we just couldn't tell anyone for fright and fear of the consequences. I should turn that on its head, I haven't wasted any time, I have been healing, rebuilding and strengthening my battlements. I have been living life the best way I know, to ensure that when that moment is reached, I meet it with open arms and hold onto it with both hands. This moment, as I look back, it's like a revelation to me; some days I have wallowed and wondered why things happen to my friends and not me. Sometimes I am grateful that I can live a pretty independent and at times solitary existence. That is me. I know not to live with jealousy in my heart and mind, because my story is completely different to everyone else's. We do what we do to get by. All of us. Every single one of us connected, even though we don't know it, through thoughts and mind. None of us have wasted any of our time, because time is something different to us all. I spent some of my time alone as that is what I needed for my healing. That is how I like it – it took me a long time to understand that, and that it is ok. I haven't had the big job or the family and children, I have healed and that is more important than anything.

I wanted to take a new perspective of life into the new year and suddenly 2020, my year, turned into a global pandemic. We all had to stay at home so we didn't catch COVID-19. Lockdowns and deaths reigned. Restrictions imposed on all. All for one and one for all. I still wanted to approach my new outlook on life with light and strength, and whilst some days are harder than others, every day is another day further from the past and is another day of happiness and bliss. So, we had to live our lives very differently suddenly, we had gone from having every freedom to being locked down. We were only allowed to leave our houses for essential work, shopping and medication or medical appointments. People had to stay two meters apart when queuing for anything and shops were limiting the number of items people could buy due to panic buyers. Why they brought all the toilet roll I will never know, but buy it they did. It was a very strange time to be alive. At the point of writing this, I wouldn't even know if I'd contract it and if I would survive. Would everyone I know be around once it was all over? The world has never experienced such a huge global shift in freedoms and rights – people who have it must be quarantined and so would have no rights. They are dying alone as their family are not allowed near them, due to it being so contagious. Mass graves would be built in some countries. New hospitals shooting up to cope with the strain on the NHS. The fear was real and undeniable, although it still didn't compare to how I felt many, many years before that. It was almost as if I had been preparing to stay at home and isolate as much as I could. It was a time for self-reflection and to grow and nurture our own spirits, find our souls, and work together to beat the common enemy. We are all in our homes, either with family or alone, dreaming. Dreaming of how we used to live. Our independence and our freedoms. Dreaming of the things we would all want to do when we could finally leave our houses and be free. Dreams.

Everyone has dreams, everyone has hope, these are the things that bind us as people. We all want to believe in something, a positive force, a God, whatever, each of these serves the same means... hope. We dream of a brighter future for our families, ourselves, everyone. Is this whole life just a pleasant dream to help us escape from the escalating conflicts within the world? I don't know. Living in a time when there is not enough love, not enough hope or a dream for the future, when we stand on a precipice with the whole world about to change through our own man-made actions. This ever changing near dystopian society seems to get more lost and darker every single day. This world we invade and control. Everyone hopes for that bright future, that goal to be fulfilled, settled and happy. Everyone has dreams and these vary greatly.

Most people dream every night. It is a nocturnal act. Many remember their dreams, many don't. I have always remembered my dreams in vibrant detail, some faded more quickly than others, some have stayed with me hauntingly. To not remember my dreams would be such a let-down to me, like a life lived, but forgotten with the rottage of age. Images of reflection and daily sorting lost, due to a lack in the capacity of memory. Then there are others who don't want to remember their dreams. Some people are haunted by their past in those dreams, nightmares they can't escape. Numbing their pain and getting out of their heads any way they can to stop them seeing images, past recollections of things they can't change or face up to. Some people say they never dream – I like to think that they just don't recall them. This, to me, seems like living a life without any music. There must always be the Yin to the Yang, the good to bad. That is how the world works. I have learnt to take the good with the bad, the smooth with the rough. All of this builds our life experience and it makes us who we are.

Dreams can be a means of escape. Some believe dreams can warn you by sending you subtle or not so subtle messages. Whatever they are, they have to originate somewhere. There must be a dream sector embedded somewhere deep inside the brain. Some dreams are so vivid that it is almost as if you are living these events in real life and when you wake up you realise it's not real. Sometimes the emotion is so strong and focused that it must be real. What if the waking time was not reality, and dreams were. Who can say? Some people who escape through their dreams may find the dream state a comfier alternative to a terrible home life, upbringing or any traumatic event in their lives. Most people have been to the dark place, most come back. Others decide to stay.

Where there are dreams, there come nightmares. This is the Yin to the Yang. Nightmares, like dreams, can take on any form that your subconscious chooses and can terrify a person in the most disturbing of ways. Sometimes the thing we are afraid of facing is ourselves. Some people then fear sleep in case of bad dreams, others are driven mad by terrible nightmares. They say if you die in a dream, you die in reality. I don't know where I stand on this, but every time I've had a dream where I've been near death, for example falling, or once when I was being eaten by wolves, I woke up just in time. Some people believe that dreams, nightmares, in whatever form can be warnings. Prophetic may be a better word. There are people who would pass it as complete balderdash, but if people can open their closed minds for twenty-seven seconds, then what scientific restraints are there to what can't be done? I don't know what I believe, but I feel like dreams have some sort of mysterious explanation just waiting to be discovered.

In some cases, people have been known to have dreams, then as pieces of them are acted out in reality, the pieces fit together and they are suddenly enlightened with whatever knowledge it is that was required for that moment. Is it possible to know what is to come? Does this mean everything we do, no matter how hard we try to change the outcome, that everything is destined to happen? If dreams can be prophetic, are they sent to us to allow us to change things or will we remain passive to the outcome? No matter what we do, are we fated to what will happen? These are questions surely no one can understand.

In terms of prophetic dreams, some believe what's going to happen, is going to happen; it is predetermined, fate. Whatever you do, you cannot change the outcome, karma will rule. I don't know if I believe in fate or karma, I've experienced too many things and seen too many bad people not get their comeuppance. Why would people dream these things if they weren't meant to be changed? Even though there is no logical reason to how people could even dream of the future – it's crazy talk surely?

Scientifically, dreams can be explained away as the subconscious sorting through material of the day. Science would tell you there is no real meaning to dreams, it's almost like a computer sorts data. People have been known to have a real sense of time during their sleep, but I'm no scientist. I believe in theology and prophecy, so I'm bound to try and convince you that dreams can be real, prophetic. Scientists would have you believe that when you dream, during rapid eye movement, your dreams last a few seconds... well, you believe what you want. I have had dreams that seem to last all night and I have a sense of time within them. Lucid dreaming. Some people can control their dreams in all aspects, I haven't mastered this skill.

I don't have a religion myself, but if people want to believe in something, they have every right to. Some cultures believe good dreams are from God and bad dreams are from Satan, other people in diverse cultures go on dream walks, they lucid dream daily. There are so many variations in belief from country to country, culture to culture, that there must be something in it, somewhere. We can only obsess and explore where dreams come from and why. It appears dreams are one of the mysteries of life that we may never understand; the subtle messages or means of escape they may keep in their detail will intrigue humanity until its end.

So here is where I tell my story, a re-enactment of dreams, some not so sweet, some beautiful. An insight into hidden worlds, submerged in the mind, experiences I have decided to share so that I can move on with my life in my own time. This is my story. I had such beautiful memories of being a very small child. My earliest memory is an extremely hazy one, I don't even know what age I would have been, but I am sure I remember being in the attic in "Erica", our first home. I distinctly remember playing Hungry Hippos in the attic with my sister Laura, and just laughter and childhood innocence echoing all around us. Light. Everything I remember is how I recall it. Other family members may remember things differently, but it is all about my own perspective. How I saw events.

The main bulk is completely and brutally honest. Names have not been changed to protect the abusers who have had so much influence over my life. Why should I have changed anything? I had nothing to hide. I had always known that I did nothing wrong and I am not weak anymore, I am strong and I can call people out for what they are, and explain my life in detail. This is like an expression and cleansing of my own soul before I move on into a happier world. A place I have spent years getting to. A place I never thought I would be, but here I am – finding my feet and finding my freedom.

Chapter 1

Sun, Sand, See Monsters

He had a dream,
I heard him say,
You don't say what you mean,
So, I will escape

<u>1984</u>

Randy Crawford, "One day I'll fly away", was playing on the stereo, a great big three-tiered heavy item with massive booming speakers. A man, his name Trevor, came storming up the hallway, face angered and flushed maroon. "Crunch", the man's fist met with the woman's face, shattering the jawbone instantly. The woman, Sharon, fell to the floor screaming in pain as the splinters of bone dug their way deep into the swelling mess. She tried to flee with her two children, a boy of one and a half years and a daughter of five years.

"If you take these kids, I will shoot them, and you, with a shotgun", sneered Trevor, eyes dark and demonised. "If you even so much as try, you will never see them again!", he swept the two children away from their crying mother. He was holding a knife in his hand and slowly waving it from side to side, his eyes psychotic.

"Flyyyyy away, one day, I'll fly."

She could do nothing but make guttural cries that echoed through the hallways of the once family home, as the two children cried, older clutching the younger as their brutal father coaxed them away from their mother. These tears would last a lifetime. Sharon fled, running miles to her parents, paranoid that Trevor was following behind with his shot gun to kill her. The two children screaming in horror as Trevor screamed at them to get upstairs to their rooms, Laura pulling the small boy up as they went.

Time slowly moved on and I have no memory of what happened over the next couple of years, but I have since learnt the truth from family members, both past and present. I am sure I would have picked up learnt behaviour from this horror show of a man, but it would be so ingrained that I would not recognise it for years, if ever. The music changed to Gloria Estefan, "The Rhythm is gonna get you", as time flowed on through 1987 to 1988.

The fact that Sharon had left her two children behind, pained her every single day, but what else could she do? He was everywhere, all the time, he even tapped on the window of her parents' spare bedroom with his shotgun one night. He did all this to terrify her and to remind her that he was still watching her as she slept in her parents' house, beyond scared.

Trevor was a terrible man, brutal in nature and unrelenting. He was born in 1946 and had a harsh upbringing. You would imagine someone treated that way would grow up to be different, I know that his father had beaten him and that his father had died at quite a young age from a brain tumour. Other than that, I knew very little about my own family. It was all very odd. Sometimes the cycle of abuse just continues. No one knew if there was anything in his past that could have caused such aggression, but it wasn't natural. A man should not treat anyone that way. He would think up tortures for his wife and children, mentally violent and unloving.

Sharon feared for the life of her children, as well as her own. She tried in vain to remove the two children from the grips of Trevor, but was thwarted at every step. Trevor drove Sharon insane. When they were still together, he would go out all the time, leaving her at home alone to look after the children while he met up with other women, drank and gambled. He would cheat on her constantly. He would even have sex with women in the family shed. He would tell women that his wife was his sister so that they didn't get suspicious. One woman even knocked on the door once and when confront by my mother came to her own realisation and said, "You're not his sister are you?"

He would pull the cord of the phone wire out just enough so that the phone wouldn't work when he wasn't there. He had taken a second mortgage out on the home, faking her signature and removed the chord so that the bank couldn't get through. He would then try to convince Sharon that she was just overthinking and overanxious, he did everything he could to break her down bit by bit. He thrived on treating people in such a callous way. The poor excuse for a man had even driven Sharon so mad that she thought he was poisoning her food, and friends had to bring her in meals that he hadn't prepared. Knowing what we all know now, it wouldn't have surprised me. He broke her down to such a degree that when it came to custody battles, she lost, because as she stood there in court, all she could do was hysterically cry for her children. All Trevor had to say was, "Look at that, do you really think she can look after children?". He could turn the charm on like a tap when it was beneficial to him. She didn't get custody of my sister and I, so we then lived our lives separated. Separated from anything normal. Separated from our mother and brought up with a parent who saw us only as a meal ticket and something powerful to hold over and control our mother with.

1989

The sun shone down on number 4 West Park. Kylie, "It's never too late", played quietly in the background, the music oozing out of the open kitchen window. The two children; I, Andrew, and Laura, laughed and played in the garden situated at the back of the house. The large holly tree was partially blocking the sun as we played on the long path down towards the gate next to the pear trees. The gentle summer breeze pushed the tree branches aside to let the light shine through like sparkling water. The darkness that was going to take over our lives was a million miles away. A storm that would last a lifetime and never be forgotten. We played in the sunlight, dazzled in a memory of childhood being created, that in years to come we would look fondly back on. I don't have many memories of that time but I recalled climbing in the big holly tree and climbing over into the neighbour's garden, running down the school fields and catching hundreds of ladybirds, out in nature. The path at the top of West Park went right around the school and that is how we accessed the fields. Back in those days there was a caretaker and I remember sitting there, crying when he came running up shouting. Further down the lane there was a darker, more overgrown part that you could climb over and hide between the fence and the path. I was always afraid that there were monsters in there, so I steered clear of it for a long time. I would run past it as quickly as I possibly could.

On the back gate of No. 4 was a sign saying, "Beware of the Children". There was a common theme of there being monsters in various places, but that was a very childish, innocent way to view things at a young age. I had no experience and no knowledge, so every single unknown was scary. I also remembered being afraid of something lurking in the washroom outside where the washing machine lived, I would run out and back as quickly as I could in case something got me. It all seemed like a hazy dream, discoloured and bright. This is the place it all began. Where I first saw things, heard things, felt things. Some people would put it down to childhood fears and anxiety, no-one would know the truth of how real monsters could be, and what would make it worse was that the monsters would not be strangers.

2019 – Present Day

The hues of colour separated as the sun set in the sky. Blue to purple, purple to red, to orange as I watched on, silhouetted in the dying light. The flowers on the ground around me were all dead. I didn't have time or need to worry about that right now. I turned my back on the sunset, lifted my head and saw it was still daylight. I spun around on the spot, one hundred and eighty degrees. The beautiful sunset I had just witnessed was gone – had it even been there, I suddenly thought to myself.

The sun now shot rays of light through the space of time, they connected with the earth in a blaze of heat and glory that rained down on me from the heavens above, sent through from the darkest recesses of space. I felt warm in its ethereal glow. For some reason, the sunlight seemed more focused and intense where I stood, like it was glaring down only on me. A spotlight on me and my life in that moment. This is my story, my dreams. At this exact moment in time, I am a thirty five year-old man. I have lived half a life. I felt that half my life ago, I was in the constraints of pain from childhood traumas. Processing everything that had happened to me, it has taken to this day to heal. I never knew then that I was so desperately unhappy, living life in such a depression caused by the events that had happened to me. I see it now. That is why I can heal and move on. I can look back now and see the long road and the slow journey it has taken in my years of recovery. I am just me, as I have always been. I don't pretend to be anything I am not and this is a story I am telling so that some may not feel so alone. If one person can read this and feel the way I have felt, and can get some hope that they too will one day get through it, then it will be worth it. This is my way of cleansing everything I have kept inside for so long, releasing it into the air like a balloon and watching it float away. I will always be connected to it, but it will no longer affect me. We all go through tough things. All of us. I have always lived in Cornwall, although it wasn't always the most relaxed place for me to live in, it was home. I grew up here and was not leaving for anyone. It's hard to describe how beautiful Cornwall is to anyone who doesn't live here; the pure green seas, totally clear and lush, the rocky outcrops where the castles stand, aged and worn down by the passage time, but full and mysterious in their beauty. The empty overgrown engine houses of the Cornish history past, the glistening sea and golden beaches – there is no better place to be when the sun is shining. People cooling themselves in the endless ocean, basking in the sun, casting themselves gently into the sea like the basking sharks who only make fleeting visits to the seas in the area. Then there would be the winter storms. The Yin to the Yang. The balance that we all need in our lives, like the good and the bad. Happy and sad. Up and down. It goes on.

1999 - Asleep in time

I walked along the beach on my own, I wondered how I came to be there, but didn't question it for long. The thought just drifted away, lost in a moment of distraction. I walked past a little house on the left that was lined with driftwood creations, obviously made by the artistic owner. Contorting, sea worn trees and various animal shapes completed from the driftwood. The beach stretched for miles, it seemed to stretch to the horizon and beyond. I always thought it was incredible even though I saw it very often, almost every day. There was something desert and oasis like in the view, something drawing and shimmering on the horizon. The golden yellowness of the sand was almost blinding, the light reflected brilliantly into my eyes. I closed them to try and stop the glare. I recall thinking how the sand close to the water's edge seemed to move like liquid against the gently lapping sea. The way the ground liquefies during an earthquake. The shoreline and land merged into one as if blurring in the brightness. It was so shiny, everything was so bright, like reflections of memories. Those brighter days when we had no cares, no stresses.

Tourists and holiday makers had set up an army of multicoloured wind-breaks and towels, all laid out like seals hauled out to breed, they basked trying to make the most of their holiday and get a nice suntan. I found it amusing, but at the same time a bit odd, as none of them appeared to be moving and were all becoming increasingly sun burnt. They remained there as if frozen in a snapshot of time. I chuckled to myself at the thought that none of them had any concept of sun cream and would probably contract skin cancer in their later years. One woman was so red, she looked like a lobster does after it has been boiled. She must have been in terrible agony but still refused to give up her prime position on the beach. Frozen there on the towel she lay as if she was immobile in time and I was looking at a photograph, her face was as red as a cherry tomato and all her loose skin oozed out of her bikini – it wasn't an attractive sight at all.

Even though the day was excruciatingly hot, I didn't appreciate that my whole attire was totally unsuitable, but I didn't care, I didn't even notice. Dressed in black on such a hot day was surely a cause for concern. Again, I was distracted from this by nothing in particular, I just continued dreamily along the beach. So dazzling. I stopped, stood still, paused for a second and decided to sit in the sand and rest my weary legs before continuing. Something internal told me to rest just for a moment. Just a second. There was no conscious thought, it just was. The sand was warm to the touch and caressed my bare hands, moulding to my shape. There was an imposing feeling as if someone had pulled the rug out from underneath me and my stomach dropped. I began to feel heavy and uneasy. A shadow flitted past me so fast it was like a blink. Was it a bird flying overhead and casting a shadow? I looked up. The sky was cloudless.

I felt a quiver of angst shoot through my stomach again, a sharp pain that felt like a small shallow cut. Something was coming, brewing, but it was so brilliant and hot, what could there be? On this perfect day, the sun sparkling off the sea, casting rainbows in rock pools, I had a sudden feeling that something dark was after me and I needed to leave immediately. Something gripped the inside of my heart and squeezed. I got to my feet as if by magic and started to move. I heard hissed words echoing around me in the thinning air. The sun intensified. "How doesss thisss feel?" a voice hissed,

"You can never escape me," it snorted, "Never escape!".
"What, huh?" I exclaimed.

I spun around looking in a three-hundred-and-sixty-degree circle. Every direction covered. There was no distinction to the voice. I could only see a slight shadow, as if not part of this dimension. I watched as it seemed to flit from rock to rock in the form of a dark shadow. It lasted less than a second at each jump so I could not tell what it was. It didn't seem to have a solid form, just a dark silhouette of a shape. I knew it was humanoid. I just knew it. I wanted to look away and to leave but appeared to be stuck on the surface of the sand now. My legs felt heavy, tired and it was like I was unable to lift them. I was drawn to the sun with a strange curium.

"Who are you?!", I demanded whilst almost blind in the sunlight. It was more of a question set with a hint of unsureness. "I will kill you!" retorted the voice, now more distant and getting further away. The feeling of curiosity and fear increased, it was like a car crash when you drive past it on the road, you want to look away, but you can't help but look. My feet unglued from the ground with a jolt and I ran towards the voice. As I ran after the eerie figure, I thought that it was a terrible idea, but didn't stop. Something inside told me to stop and kept on shouting, "No, no, no", but I didn't. There wasn't much of a thought process, it was like a momentary thought that dissipated as soon as it appeared. A fraction of a second.

Suddenly I approached the cliff face, I was so preoccupied with... well, I didn't really know – I had forgotten about the shadow and the chase. It was as if I just seemed to be drifting as if in a morphine induced dream. I kept coming to myself and then I would be gone again. It was a very strange and unsettling feeling, also confusing, but it was still so sunny. Brilliant brightness and clear skies. The heat and light were intensifying and increased my confusion. The sun continued to glow ever stronger in the midday sky, as it reflected off of the sand at certain points over the rolling beach, it flashed temporarily, blinding me each time.

"I could get rid of you any time I like...", whispered a voice, "Anytime...". I turned around on the spot and looked up, I didn't know where the voice came from, but was sure it was the shadowy thing I had seen. An object that I did not, could not at the time, or didn't wish to give a specific name. The ground beneath my feet trembled. No, I thought to myself, it must have just been a twitch in my leg as I continued along the edge of the cliff face, heading into the cooling shade that had appeared. Before this, there had been no differentiation in light, it had only been an intense vivid light. Now there were small black spots appearing, cooling shade that looked to provide relief. I didn't even think it was strange that all of the people once stationary like a Polaroid, had all disappeared. The beach was clear.

As I turned, the sight that greeted me nearly overwhelmed me. It may have only been in my eyesight for three seconds and no more, but it was a face. A twisted face that I would never forget. It appeared to have been a man, his face was badly mutilated with a large laceration to what was a rotting left cheek. On the other side, the cheek area had sunken in and his eyes were a deep red. Blood soaked the man's face and his hair had stuck and matted to it in areas. There was a large circular hole near the top of his head and there was a greyish piece of brain bulging out. I felt that my stomach would heave and I would throw up there and then on the beach. How embarrassing.

"You!", an invisible voice shouted into my ear, "Hahaha", it laughed, squealing in delight. "We will become one," it continued, hissing incessantly just out of my sight. All I felt was fear. The dreamy sense and the feel of the heat suddenly turned cold, like someone had frozen my blood dead in my veins. I didn't know what to do and didn't really understand, but all I knew was that whatever it was following me and taunting me, wasn't good. It wanted me gone. So I began to run again, this time with huge steps. Taking huge leaps and bounds to get away from this entity. My lunges becoming bigger and bigger as I tried to make ground. As I ran, small pebbles began to fall from the cliff face above and roll towards me as I tried to get nearer to the shoreline. The shoreline appeared safe to me, but as I accelerated towards it, it was getting farther and farther away from me, as if the waves were going backwards. Sanctuary getting further away. The cool relief of the water slowly ebbing away. A few small fragments started to hit me and I felt a grape sized stone hit me in the middle of the forehead, which really hurt. The pain was momentary.

The ground trembled beneath my feet again. There was no denying it this time. Definitely a deep kind of rumble that had nearly knocked me, the fleeing man, off of my feet. The beach seemed to stretch on and on, the sun grew brighter and more dazzling. I had to put my arm over my face to protect my eyes from the ever-increasing glare. I ran in and out of the shadows based at the edge, looking for some sort of protection from the heat. I felt small branches push out from the cliff face, which forced me to dart back out into the sun, it felt like it was burning through my skin and down to the bone. Constantly on the run from an invisible force of some kind, I didn't see the dark shadow that flickered in and out of sight behind me. The shape was dark and would be in one spot for less than a second before it disappeared, and would reappear again slightly nearer to its target. I didn't see any of this. I didn't see it approaching, but I remember I was trying to find something, flee from something or get somewhere, but the thoughts kind of melted away in the heat like ice cream.

I came to a standstill and as I panted, trying to get my breath, I put my hands on my knees. I took in deep lungs full of the fresh, but hot air. I looked up and thought it was such a bright, hot day – the brightest I had seen. Déjà vu. Just there. There was a feeling of uncertainty, but I knew that it was completely natural to feel like this and that no matter what happened, I would be okay. All that mattered was that the sun was shining down on me, on that day, in that moment in time. I had forgotten about the darkness and the fear, and the small pebbles that were now falling behind, getting bigger and moving faster. I felt like I was meant to be there, at that time, in that moment, I couldn't explain why. I had always believed in something like fate or destiny. I was never religious but guessed everything must happen for a reason, and if that's the case, you may as well just chill out and go with the flow. What's going to happen will happen.

The ground shifted again, this time I saw the sand open up ahead of me and expose a deep hole. This was quickly filled by the sand as if sliding gracefully into the hole like a waterfall of gold. The shaking continued and I could do nothing but stay on the spot and go with the movement. I remembered how far I had been running, but now my feet were stuck again. Not glued, but as if I wasn't even really trying to lift them. I remembered the people frozen to the spot as if in the Polaroid picture. The sand flowed like a river. Meandered like water. I didn't feel as if it had been more of a destination than to fill the hole I had seen. My thoughts were so disconnected. Every thought and every memory just seemed to last a second, then disappeared. Lost forever. Forgotten as soon as they formed

The sand was now moving upwards, I felt drunk as if I had been missing moments in time. I felt like Icarus being pushed up too close to the sun, feeling slightly panicked as it was getting hotter and hotter. I remember pulling my top off in hopes that I may feel the cooling breeze against my skin. It was so hot I could instantly feel my skin turning a shade of red. The river of sand pushed me upwards continuously towards the hot sun. I swayed around on the spot awkwardly, as if my feet had been trapped in merciless black tar. I felt that if I tried to pull away, I would be sucked in deeper; the growing mass of sand continued to push me up higher and higher, faster and faster. These exaggerated sand dunes grew and grew until I was balanced upon the edge of a ledge, so high that I could see the sea below and a small seal. It looked as tiny as a pin prick. Everything below was so small, so far away. I thought that if I fell from such a height, I would surely die. Then I heard the laugh again and felt that familiar surge of fear.

From this height I could see everything, bathed in bright luscious sunlight. The sand had stopped shifting and I was at the top of a huge hill of sand, a mountain. I was perched on a solid ledge of sand that felt as if it could disintegrate at any moment. The sun was so bright, so hot, glowing. The blue of the sea looked warm and inviting, but it was now so far down and far away that it looked like a still rockpool waiting to be disturbed by inquisitive children looking for sea creatures. I recall thinking how deep it would be if I were to dive in, then remembered my feet were stuck in the invisible tar. Trapped on the spot and unable to hold onto a thought, emotion or feeling for more than a few seconds. The feeling of dread suddenly kicked in again. This made me feel menaced and unnerved, I tried to turn around to see what was approaching. I was filled with a sense of foreboding, what would happen if the massive sand mountain just collapsed? Or what if it kept growing, surely in this heat, I'd die? What if the laughing voice caught up with me? It was a feeling of fear in the pit of the stomach that didn't go away. This feeling would remain for some time to come.

A sudden pain seared through my body, I tried again to spin around on the spot, clawing at my back where I had already taken my shirt off. Something had scratched me on the lower part of the back. From what I could see, the scratch was about six inches long and I winced as I ran my finger along the perfect slice. I couldn't see it well, but I could tell it was quite deep. The blood appeared on my fingers, so I knew it was a fresh cut as it takes a few seconds for the flow to begin. Where did this come from? Who did this? The shadow passed again at speed. I felt as if something evil was there, I couldn't say what it was, but I felt darkness and sensed an eerie aura to the air around me. I stared up into the sun and all I could see was black spots where it had momentarily blinded me. Still thinking how ethereal the light was, but now it was taking on a sinister feel – it was too hot. I felt like my eyeballs were burning. Water was trying to stream to keep them moisturised, but it was in vain. I felt there was something coming after me. I felt pushed down and as if my energy was being fed upon. If only I had known it was a real monster, something I couldn't escape even if I tried.

As I looked down towards the beach again, I could make out faint sights. The sand shifted again and dropped a bit, so I was suddenly closer. It was vertically below me now, there were small poles that looked like barber shop poles, all brightly coloured red, white and blue. It took a few moments of confusion for me to realise that there were people hanging on to them, their mouths were moving frantically, legs kicking for invisible ground, fingers gripping as tightly as possible to hold on. I heard no sound from their mouths, just gaping crevices. I could hear nothing. And it was still so bright, white hot light. Their silent pleas would go unanswered, as one by one I watched them lose their grip and fall. Their fingers slipping as they tried to hold on. Faces contorted, struck with horror. I was unable to help them; all I could do was watch. I held my breath and tried to turn my head to my shoulder, but I was frozen, like a bug in amber. A realisation dawned on me; I was frozen like one of those Polaroid picture people baked by the hot sun into a moment that would last for eternity. Melting, fading like pictures left on windowsills when exposed to light for long periods of time.

I heard the sinister laugh again echoing somewhere in the distance, it sounded cruel and vicious. I want to be able to fly away. Like the song, "Wind beneath my wings", I'd just fly away to find my hero. Someone to save me from this…this dream? The sand beneath my feet began to shift again, I watched it circling away under me as if I was inside a giant hourglass. The sky was vast and cloudless, the sun continued to beat down, casting its own unblinking eye down on me, never letting me out of its sight for one moment. The sand continued to pour away onto the boiling beach below. My feet were glued to the spot there was nothing I could do; I don't even recall if I could move my eyes. It was still so bright, everything just glowed blindingly. My eyes widened in horror as the sand suddenly disappeared and I went into freefall, hurtling towards the age-old beach below. I thought, "This will end quickly. Please let it be quick and painless".

The sea was still sparkling. I thought to myself that I should be making an urgent effort to somehow stop myself, but that thought faded away instantly.

I was falling farther and farther, but the ground didn't seem to be getting any closer. I thought this was rather odd but didn't question it further than that. It was almost like a constant amnesia and as soon as a memory or thought formed, it was gone. Everything reset. So, the moments of horror that came along with the fear, the laughter and everything, felt new to me every time. I didn't want to hit the ground like one of those people I had seen fall just now, broken bodies bombarding the beach below. I envisaged myself clawing for some sort of edge that would save me. I imagined the pain of me grasping for roots, branches, anything, and the pain that would cause. Fingernails torn. There was nothing though, I just kept falling. I seemed to be falling forever, I couldn't understand what was going on. The sun still beamed down and I smiled as I forgot all of my thoughts and became one with this beautiful light. It encapsulated me. Beautifully intensifying.

"I wonder if...", I said to myself as I was suddenly consumed by the sand and ground, disappearing out of sight in a single momentary glimpse. I felt no pain. felt nothing or thought anything. I just fell like a cannonball into the sand, lungs choking on the warm darkness. I felt wet. I looked up and could see the sun glinting above me. I was under water. How did I get here? Water encapsulated me. I felt the urgency of wanting to suddenly breath. I didn't feel anything. The water was warm. I attempted to swim up towards the light, arms back and kicking my feet as hard as I could. I was longing to take a breath, struggling to get to the top before my air ran out. "Huuuuh," was the sound that I made as I broke free at the surface of the water.

Flicking my dark hair back, I thought it most strange that I would be in water, as I wasn't the biggest fan of deep, open water. In fact, I was quite averse to it. At the surface, the bright sunlight had gone now and I was in pitch blackness. I had been afraid of the dark for a long time. I had always been afraid of what lurked in the dark, hiding in the shadows before coming and doing something unspeakable to me. I didn't know if ghosts or demons were real, but I did believe in monsters, real ones. And I knew of a real monster.

The water lapped around me, black and impenetrable. My eyes were not adjusting to the dark at all, so I swam forward, straining my eyes whilst searching for some sort of ripple, shallow area or a ledge. Instead, I came up against a massively tall wall, its consistency was black red rock and felt slimy to the touch. I felt something in my gut that gave me fear. I always knew I should have listened to my instincts. I didn't like this and pulled back from it, uneasy. I was starting to get cold. What had happened to the beautiful sun and that... I stopped, frozen for a second... that thing, that voice. Those people. I began to remember what had happened and my insides twisted, stomach knotted. I felt ill with the reality of the situation. The wall loomed ominously over me as I tried to convince myself that whatever had been chasing me before was gone, and that in a moment I would come to an edge. I could grab hold of it and get out of what appeared to be a huge, circular pool, lake or inlet of some sort. It could have been the sea; it was so big I just didn't know. Then as soon as I approached the wall, it sunk. Hope sunk with it. I didn't know what was happening, this place was dark. It was endless. There was nothing solid. I feared what would find me. Or even if there was anything else out there, I was just trapped in a dark, endless, liquid void. There were no crashing waves nor sounds of sea birds. Nothing. It was silent except for the sound of my own splashing and the dull thud of my pulse. I felt like I could feel it in my ears. Throbbing.

There was no refuge from the water as the coldness began to take hold of me. Although there was no light, my eyes felt slightly adjusted to the darkness and I thought how smooth and seamless the water seemed, almost thick like honey. I didn't notice the light below me at first, but suddenly I began to feel very warm. A little too warm. That kind of warm when you exercise a little too hard and have a slight panic attack when you get stuck in your T-shirt. Almost that sort of warmth you get when you come over feeling sick just before you get the saliva in your mouth. The light grew from the size of a penny and distant to the size of a football and much closer, then it seemed to fill the whole underneath in a dull light. This light was a mixture of white and yellow hues, emanating from below. I looked down and saw it. I could see the wall really far below surrounded by the light – it looked like it was dissolving.

A surge of fear pulsed through my veins and my heart pounded. Adrenaline surged. I was sure I felt something brush my leg under the water. I pulled my leg away as there was a second sort of tug on it. The light filled the whole pool now, glowing menacingly through the black water and lighting up my face. I couldn't see anything in the light, but I remembered the hideous laugh I had heard earlier, that bright sun seemed like such a long time ago, like it was a dream. I was frozen in fear. I didn't want to make a commotion in the water as that may attract whatever I thought was there. A hand suddenly emerged from the water, I didn't have time to see if it was male or female, dead or alive. It was so quick. It grabbed me with such a force, that I yelped out in shock and pain. Then I saw another arm. The second arm was withered and in the bright white glow, I could see chunks of it missing. It was decaying and appeared to be doing so before my very eyes; flakes of skin peeling away like leaves falling from trees and blowing in the wind, time seemed to slow down. I had never felt such terror, such utter fear. Ancient trepidation. I continued to watch in slow-motion and terror as small flakes of grey skin fell off, then a huge flap of skin, revealing bone beneath. The white and now hot water bubbled ferociously around me as I let out a long and petrified scream. Another arm grabbed my shoulder from behind, I turned throwing it off, trying to escape in the water, trying to get away. More hands grabbed at my clothing, my skin beneath felt as if it was being stretched on my bones, clamping on with unnatural ease. The paranormal yellowy, white, hot light pulsed slowly as it engulfed everything in sight – it's light seemed to cast no shadow nor show any sign of land or a clue as to where I was lost. I saw myself from above as if I was getting further away. The blackness of the water was filling with the light, blinding me as I surveyed myself from above in the middle of the water. More arms clung to me like animals' teeth gripping skin during a feeding frenzy. I felt the pain and dread as I was suddenly pulled under water, fast and deep. I looked up to see the light that had engulfed me, was now above me. It got farther and farther away until it became a pinhead. Then the pinhead of light became darker and darker, and then there was no breath, no air... nothing.

Chapter 2

In the beginning

The childhood gripes,
The unspoken rain,
Everything will come to good
When the sun shines again

<u>2019</u>

I opened my eyes. I don't remember what age I was when I felt the change. The turn of my mind. The one thing that I knew was that I'd never forget. I could completely forgive now, but not forget. Certain things that happen etch irreversible marks on your mind. People get hurt and left behind, others remain on the outside and blind to what's going on around them.

I always knew more should have been done, but I was indifferent to it all now – that had been an awfully long time ago. The events that have made me who I am will never leave, but I always knew, always, that it was never my fault. I had been weak at times, like everyone, and I realised one day in the not so distant past, that I am human. I am not like those two. Them. I can only be the person I had to become to protect myself and endure the trials that only few dare to think about. Unbelievable things. I can tell you, but you may not want to believe. You may not want to look.

I had always known that I wanted to tell my story, I just didn't know how. It didn't feel right and I did feel shame and anger for a long time. As that ebbed away, I became stronger. I wondered who would believe it, if anyone would add things up and release what myself and my sister had been put through as children. They do say abused children grow up to be dysfunctional adults. This is true, but we all do our best to heal. We don't all turn out like the abusers, our revenge is moving on and carrying on. I always thought that if I told anyone about the monsters I encountered, that they would laugh it off. I felt that no-one would believe me – I mean, a child could lie. Now with hindsight, I realised it was more because I was frightened and could never speak out against those older, more authoritative people. I now realise these two people had no soul, not even a whole one between them. There was some deep darkness within them. To brutalise a child is to have no light. No soul. Monsters.

It always sounds complicated, but to understand the complexity of an individual you have to take it right back to the start, to the root of it all. That way the problem can be solved or it will only grow. So, this is sort of where it starts. It jumps around as the mind never stays in once place for too long. Thoughts appear and disappear in a moment. However, this is all truth; I have no reason to lie. I have no reason to accuse anyone of anything, as they know who they are and what they have done. They are accountable to themselves and have to live with what they have done to myself and countless others. I owe them no judgement anymore. This is a kind of therapy; it is the healing we all need. The cages of our own minds will be our own hell, but we can escape them. I am now able express who I am and how I feel and tell the story that I wanted to tell for so many years – shout it out, because I am not ashamed and I never should have been.

4 West Park

Memories begin at untold ages, some can be vivid, others can be mere flashes triggered by a scent or returning to a place you vaguely recall being before. I had a good memory. My earliest by far was playing in the attic of "Erica", my first home, when I was no more than two years old. I had misty recollections of looking out of the huge skylight at the massive world below and hearing the German shepherd barking down below. Everything was so big, spacious. It all only looked so big because I was so small.

After this slight incision on my mind, consciousness dawned into childhood. My memory became part of the reality that we all live in; vivid, harsh and bright. From that moment when we are born, we find ways out of the negative, unstimulating situations we find ourselves in. We deal with things the best way we can to ultimately survive. My beginnings were very humble indeed, my father was a gambling man, a fierce man. My mother had fled when I was a baby, so I didn't really think of this woman as much of a mother. My sister looked after me the most. At that age, I didn't really understand – I just felt abandoned. I had my issues for a very long time, but I learnt over time what my father was like and I understood why my mother had left. In full graphic detail. She could do nothing, he had full control of all of our lives. We were all weapons and tools he could use to get what he wanted. I was so angry at my mother for so long for leaving me and my sister, Laura, with that man. However, as time went on and I got older, I empathised. My father, Trevor was a selfish man. On the outside, he had a glowing smile and told people what they wanted to hear, whilst trying to take them for everything they had. He was a dark-haired charmer, an arch manipulator. I had always seen this, even from a young age and knew it was wrong. I knew he was wrong.

I guess if people grow up with nothing then you become hardened to the struggles and don't take materialistic people too seriously. People can surround themselves with as much "stuff" as they like, but in the end that is all they have. This young boy of only four years of age was told to be grateful for what he got, before being told to stand in the corner at home for what seemed like hours. Even at a young age, I was full of wisdom and a hunger to learn. I knew that materialism led to greed and that people who are greedy hold no attraction in my eyes. I began to grow up in this second house at 4 West Park in Redruth.

I always remember the year as 1988, when I was five, as my sister Laura used to play "Buffalo stance", by Neneh Cherry all the time. I remember hearing the songs from "Dirty Dancing" and a lot of Enya, "Orinoco Flow." At the time, I thought that song was magical; I guess this was my first foray into music, where I would later escape. Laura used to take me into the garden and get me to hold an elasticated string with my feet while she attached the other end to the bin and do her skip jump routines. I was just young. No real memories or cares of anything. My bedroom was decorated in Thundercat's wallpaper – I had a Thunder Tank and even a Thundercat's lamp. Strangely enough, a He-man bedspread. The home we had was spacious, it had an honest sized front garden and a larger back garden. There was a garage with a washhouse attached to it, which I used to run from each time in case something came out and got me, like a ghost or something. I never went into the garage alone as it was full of spiders. Growing up the side of the garage was a twisted old pear tree and on the opposite side of the garden was a huge holly tree that I often scaled, getting prickles and scratches on the way. Some memories were like water colours, kind of blurry, but warm and fuzzy, nice. I used to climb over the wall into next door, where Tim and Debbie lived. My sister and I would hang out in their house; I always remember that Tim had a blue bedroom with a big Frankenstein he had painted on the wall. He was older than me, but I guess he was my first male friend. It wasn't until years and years later that I asked my sister if she ever knew what had happened to the family after we left, she sadly said that Tim had died of an overdose years before. I still remember him fondly and quite often, which is important. Just to think of the people who have passed. Really, if you think of them and picture them often, then they are never truly gone.

They always live on. The memories I have of the home are vivid. I recall the layout of the house. The circular window at the bottom of the stairs that fascinated me. In the summer, outside the back door, I would collect hundreds of ladybirds in a bowl as I played. I recall poppies growing down towards the back gate. I remember them in bloom and after the flowers had died, they turned into crispy rattles, with the seeds inside. Red and proud, the poppies stood in the sunshine, gently swaying in the breeze as that young boy played in the garden. These were good times. Maybe some of the purest and best before it all started. I have vivid recollections of running through green fields, lazy summer days, hazy times. However, all these memories were tainted because of two people; Alison, Trevor and, of course, the nightmares that started around the same time. I always knew the nightmares were part of the fears I had from what happened, but as I grew in age, I also wondered if there were other, less obvious meanings.

The first nightmares I remember, involved me waking up and not being able to move from the bed. Each time I had it there would always be a great pressure holding me down, pushing me into the soft mattress. My voice was only a hoarse croak as I screamed silently out into the darkness. I couldn't cry out for help, couldn't move or stop whatever the force was, I was completely powerless. Each time I had this dream, I woke up in pools of sweat. Occasionally, to the sickly sweet and twisted, smiling face of the evil Alison. Most of the time, I could see nothing in the smooth darkness, eyes strained and bulged in their sockets. I always remember the lingering scent that was in this nightmare, it was a mixture of sickly sweet perfume and daffodils. I didn't know why, it was just a way of describing the scent. It was totally nauseating as the putrid stench filled the air. Closing my eyes, I would try to muster all my strength and push up against the mattress; but no matter what I did, nothing helped. Sometimes the dream was a slight variant where I would be able to bang on the wall, but it was never heard. There was never a response or rescue. Suddenly peering towards the door, I would have missed it if I had my eyes shut, was a brief but definite sight of a pearly white skull. The sight of its deep, dark and empty sockets was forever etched in this small child's mind. I could never speak, but always thought, "Oh god, oh god, here it comes..." – I felt like an animal in the corner, trapped. But I had no way of fighting back, I was powerless, afraid and alone. This is a theme of emotions that would follow me for a long time.

Out of the corner of my eye, I would often see the darkness shift and alter slightly, the grip or force loosened slightly and I was able to move a bit. Though these movements felt rough and floppy. The movement became a slow swirling, the sort of motion as if a door has been left open and gusts of breeze are gently floating through the room. The twists and swirls became greyer and more obvious, curling around each other in random motions and patterns. I pulled back and squeaked in fear as a face suddenly loomed from what looked like a plume of smoke in the middle of my bedroom. It slowly floated, silently towards my face. I could feel the blood pumping through my veins, my heart exploding through my chest wall and in my temples, thumping. My head felt like it was about to overheat and explode. As a small, poor child, I had no idea what to do – I didn't even think of escape, as this was my life. It was the norm. My reality. In reality, I would be twisting in my bed, dripping with sweat at my many unseen, constant ordeals.

As quickly as it emerged, the face would be gone and I would be shaken awake. This is where the nightmare became a reality, for there was an evil more powerful than anything that a small child could imagine. The monsters under the bed, the bogeyman, this woman topped all of them with brisk ease. Brutal and cruel in the acts she dished out and incited. Acts of terrible violence towards me from the age of three years old. There would be many, many occasions of this happening over the years. I would be prompted what to say, as once again Social Services had been called by, "Some typical bastard", my dad would say. I guess my nan and grandad had reported my dad to Social Services when they saw bruises on my body – this was not an uncommon occurrence.

I used to play with my "Monsters in My Pocket" in my grandad's sheds. He used to own Trevenson Moor Garden Centre in Pool. He was a very loyal and proud man. The head of his household. The complete opposite to my dad. My glorious grandad, Douglas, was well respected by all. One of my earliest memories was playing with the cuckoo clock my grandparents had been given on their wedding day. I would pull the heavy pinecone looking attachment to try and make the clock chime. I would hear grandad say in his cockney accent,

"Bloody hell Mary, he's playing with that clock again". I would be taken on visits by my mother, when my dad allowed access. Every time we left my nan's house, I would start to go back and forth to the toilet, clearly showing signs of distress. I assume now, with perspective, that they all knew why, but there was nothing any of them could do. My father had all the power and was a terribly threatening and violent man. My mum was too mentally unable to go up against him and my grandparents only had limited power. There were moments when I was not afraid, but these were few and far between for someone of my young age. Most of the happy moments were when my mum would play songs in the car and we would all sing along, driving in the sunshine. Sonia, "You'll never stop me from Loving you" and Yazz, "The only way is up" were songs I remembered very well.

I remember my father sitting myself and my sister down and prompting us on what to say to Social Services, saying that we could be taken away. Threatening us. We were terrified, so we did as we were told. I guess my sister and I never thought of the alternative of a happy, carefree life – that didn't exist to us. I am so thankful for the moments, days and weekends we got to spend away from Trevor, as it ensured that we didn't turn out the same way as him. That little bit of respite was extremely important. We knew what love was from the people outside of that house, away from Trevor and Alison.

Most of what I remember as a child was being terrified. He withheld the visits to our mother whenever he saw fit. He spoke so ill of her that when we had visited, we had to pretend that we hadn't had a nice time. We learnt to lie and hide things at a very young age. When we came home, he would say, "Did you have a nice time?", Laura and I would have to say, "No". The reality was totally different. When we were away from 'home' we had the time of our lives. Our mum took us to all sorts of places like Flambards, we walked in the sun, we painted and drew, we sang songs and played games and music – just like children are meant to do. That's how I knew from the start that it was never mine or Laura's fault. We were never self-blamers in this situation. We knew we were the victims and that one day, we would be out of it. One day, we would get the upper hand and even if we didn't take any physical action, their own thoughts and minds would someday become their downfall and prison. I said to myself many times over the years, that I would like to see karma appear for them. We were abused children after all, and we learnt the skills of manipulation they had – these would be handy tools for later in life.

Alison began scratching the chest of drawers in my bedroom, scratching my name into the drawers. And then, tearing my Thundercat's wallpaper, breaking my Thunder Tank and my other toys. Some toys disappeared completely. That was how it started anyway. She even went as far as to destroy the first book I ever read, Moses Prince and Shepard. A story of a baby boy sent off down a river in order to escape his death. I seemed to be able to relate to this. I often dreamt of lovely families who would take me away from my life. However, each day I would wake up, stare at the same cold walls and feel the knot of fear tighten in my stomach at what the day would bring. She moved on to cutting her own clothes in my dad's wardrobe and pouring her creams into her knicker drawer. I don't even know why she had so much stuff at my dad's home, she had her own family and her own husband. From what I understood from overheard phone calls, was that he was impotent and she was... well, a cheating, nasty piece of work.

The beatings from my father became more frequent and usually had Alison in the background saying, "Please don't hurt him, Trevor", with a malicious glint in her eye. The abuse from Alison also grew. She went from slapping me in my bed to sexual abuse. She used to grab my penis and threaten to pull it off. My sister once saw this but never knew the full extent. Alison would hit me around the head and she would come into my bedroom at night and pour urine on me. I found out many years later from my sister that it was urine as it smelt like it, to make it look like I had wet the bed. My father would constantly be dragging the mattress outside to dry out in the summer. He assumed I had problems mentally. It wouldn't have been surprising considering we were used for theft and all sorts. Some of my earliest memories involved him taking me and Laura shopping. He would steal food and put items down his trousers. I remember being instilled with this at an early age and stealing the free toys out of the cereal boxes while he was off down the other aisles, stealing. Alison always hit me around the head whenever she came to the house. Some days, I thought I had got away with nothing when she was there, then suddenly I would receive a whack. And the other days it was more and more, endless. When we went out anywhere and she was there, she would squeeze my hand so tightly that I could hear crunching, but I couldn't make a scene or cry out. I didn't dare make a scene or cry out as it would result in more beatings, because I would have shown them up in public. I would have been an embarrassment. Whilst I lived at West Park, this was the total norm. There were times when I was allowed out and, in those moments, I would forget about what was going on at home, but that feeling deep down was always there waiting for when I returned. I would never know what I was returning home to. The grass of the school field at the top of my road was always so lush and green. There were red plants that grew there and I always thought that that was the only place they grew in the whole world. There was a little lane that ran right down the back of the school and down towards the road the opposite way. There was a little curved wall that led down to the road. I often crossed this on my own to play over near the train track towards St. Euny Church. That must show innocent I really was. Usually when I got home, it was for a beating or I would be forced to sit to the dining table and write lines for what seemed like hours. I got good at doing lines as I would write the first word down the whole page, then the second word and so forth. Trevor would make me sit there doing lines until my hands hurt.

They say that children mimic the behaviour of adults and I began to copy this behaviour, I think I did it in a supply cupboard at school when I was maybe six years old. I recall squirting all the toothpaste and other items in the store cupboard everywhere. I was clearly damaged from a very early age. When I was at home and sat in the lounge with the pair, Alison would say I stuck the V signs up at her with my fingers and he would agree, then beat me, so much so that I used to sit on my hands so that I couldn't be accused of anything. That didn't work. Alison was a typical, witchy sort of looking woman with long, dark hair, a roman nose and who spoke with a harsh, posh tone. Although she wasn't posh, she was actually evil incarnate. She had a dry, sarcastic tone and looked down her nose at everyone. She traumatised a young boy from three years old and it still sickens me to this day. I remember her hitting me around the head as a small boy saying, "What the fuck are you doing out of bed!?" and pushing me out of the way. This was an occasion where my mum had dropped us home and witnessed this. She and Alison got into a big fight and my sister ended up being shut in the wardrobe. The fear was constant and as time went on, I became more and more habituated to it.

Alison used to create scenarios to get me into trouble and then make out as if she wanted my father to go easy on me, like she was sympathetic or trying to help me out. Cruel and evil, calculated and unrepentant. "Oh Trevor, I don't know what you're going to do with that boy", sighed Alison, "The little fucking asshole!" screamed Trevor as he tore down the hallway, slinging open my door and grabbing me out of bed. "What have you done you little fucking bastard!" he yelled, as he began to rain blows down on the half-awake child. "Little fucking cunt", he would hiss through angry, gritted teeth. I always remember that first pain. The intensity. This pain would become a frequent guest, though never a friend. Alison was trying to convince my dad that there was something wrong with me so that she could have me sent away. "Maybe you need to go to a special school!" sniped my dad during many beatings. Lashings from belts, the buckles, slippers... anything that Trevor could lay his hands on. "When me and your father are married, you are going to boarding school", laughed Alison menacingly on many occasions.

The abuse had intensified to such a level that during one night, when I was nearly eight years old, Alison had squirted washing up liquid in the cereal cupboard and all of the cereal. When Trevor awoke in the morning, he opened the white handled brown door to see the Fairy Liquid everywhere, he exploded. He stood me in front of the sink, questioning me as to why I had done it. I was so afraid. All I could say was, "I don't know.". I honestly didn't know. I could never really compute what they wanted me to say or to admit to. "Put out your hands!" demanded my so-called dad, "No, I don't want...", I wept as a young boy. "Put them out!" screamed my dad, inches from my face. His face contorted into a monstrously angry, inhumane man. A real monster. Alison was usually in the background, glaring on with dark eyes. I could feel empathically that she was pleased. Her dark desires were being met for the moment. As I slowly moved my open palms out in front of him, "Thwack!" the belt came down with such a force and intensity it made me scream out in agony. My father launched into a frenzied attack that left me cowering in the corner after being forced towards the work top. Alison then came over to me crumpled in the corner, pulled me back up to the work top and pushed me as close to without being on it. She was then holding my hands down as Trevor went over to the sink, got the bottle of Fairy washing up liquid. He squirted some into a cup and put in water to the top. He then cruelly said, "You want to put this on the cereal, then you drink it!". He then force-fed me the watered down washing up liquid. I never forgot this moment. Not all the scars heal. They lessen with time, but experiencing events like that at such a young age had a huge impact on me. I was distant at school. Falling asleep at school, probably due to being awake all night in fear of them doing something to me. Trevor was a vicious and extremely quick-tempered man. Alison's eyes glowed happily often in the corner. Whenever my father and Alison would fight, he would take it out on me afterwards. Or if he stormed out of the house, leaving her there, she would come upstairs and pull my hair, pull my penis or slap me in my bed. I never fully slept for the fear of who would be coming into my bedroom. This equated to one very tired, but also severely matured child.

When I learnt to ride a bike up and down the lane, Alison would push me off if she had the opportunity. Or if she arrived to visit my dad, she would lie and say she had seen me down by the main road, where I had been specifically told not to go. Each time, I was either made to do hundreds of lines or I was beaten. Sometimes both. Trevor would force me to call him, "sir" and make me clean the house, do all the chores, pick up dogshit. What sort of person does that to a child? I should have been enjoying life not living in such fear. I lived in this house until 1991 and the abuse had continued throughout the whole time that I was there.

The most horrific and defining moment came when we went on a local holiday. I recall us going on a holiday to a chalet in Hayle. They played, "Let's do the Time Warp" and I had a photo taken with a girl from school called Penny Hollywood. We were in the swimming pool on a big crocodile. It reminded me of the Roald Dahl book, The Enormous Crocodile. It's funny what you remember. What I also remember is Alison and her usual hand squeezing technique. The cracking of the hand. This time, she did something that crossed even more lines. I clearly remember her laying back and making me kiss her private area. She said if I didn't, she would pull my willy off again. She would then pull and twist it. I never thought she grabbed me in a sexual way but to inflict pain and control. I never even considered telling my father. Who would believe a small child? He wasn't the sort of understanding father, so I remained silent. For years. My father did not come across as a sympathetic man and he wouldn't have believed me. That was probably the worst act she carried out on me. I wondered if I would ever have the courage to stand up to her, tell her what she had done. Tell her that I made it through.

We had a dog and I remember when we got her, she was such a small, cute, little ball of fur. Our dog Sasha was a beautiful German Shepherd. She once tore up the kitchen dining area and my dad went mental. There was fluff from cushions and foam everywhere. He beat the dog. He also beat me. When I was in too much pain to eat, he made me sit at the table for hours and hours and hours. I learnt acts of defiance from these two people. I guess I learnt how to lie, charm and manipulate just like them. Both myself and my sister learnt this very well. We could even trick my father into thinking we hadn't done things when at our mother's. I was always told by my dad that I was on punishment when I went to my mum's and therefore wasn't allowed sweets and television. However, my mum ignored this. When Laura and I would go and visit our mum, it was like a relief. A few days away. Although when it was time to return, I used to run to the bathroom as per usual and not want to come out. I would feel ill. This was not normal behaviour for a child. I was sure my mother used to pick up on this and would sing songs with us all the way home, to try and brighten the mood – "Ging Gang Goolie" was a favourite. Regardless of this, I never wanted to go home to my father. Never wanted to see his face again. I just wanted to stay in the peace and tranquillity of my mum's house. Returning home to the tyrant and his evil apprentice was my biggest fear. Not the monsters or ghosts in the dark I dreamt of. They never came close. Trevor was such a well-practiced deceiver that he would represent himself in court. He exuded charm that meant he could get anyone to do anything he wanted. He had everybody fooled. I just seemed to accept what was happening, because what could I do? I was merely a child and these two adults were severe and violent. I feared for my life and became habituated to the pain. I was in constant fear. My sister and I would never know what we were returning home to. I probably even got angry at school with other children – the cycle of abuse and all that.

It was at this age of about eight years old, that I started to feel like there were other people there sometimes. It was more a feeling of a presence or something I could feel with my body, but I didn't understand it. I got a sensation of tingling. I didn't really know what a ghost was, but I thought it was some kind of monster. I knew that monsters weren't real. Except for those human ones. In the house we lived in, there were certain places I didn't want to go at certain times, because I was worried that I may see 'something'. I didn't know what this meant at the time, it could have been a manifestation of the constant fear that I was experiencing, like I was constantly waiting for something to happen. Maybe causing it myself, the way they say poltergeists are born out of energy. I did often wonder if I was just going insane from the abuse and looking for a way out of my own body, my own life. Separating from myself.

"Don't be so hard on the boy", Alison would mutter quietly as she watched wide-eyed from the hallway. Her voice was monotone, uncaring and devoid of any real human emotion. There was no empathy in her towards me, a small defenceless child. I always wondered what Laura and I had done to her to make her treat us this way. We were a threat to her relationship with our father. The truth is our mere existence threatened her. She peered into the lounge, watching the act of violence. My sister told me various things about how calculating and evil Alison was. She would give my sister gifts. Alison would then sneak into the house when no one was there, steal the gifts back and then when she would next visit, she would ask my sister where the gift was, and my sister would be unable to find it. The abuse was physical, mental and emotional. The sexual abuse I experienced didn't happen very much and after the holiday park it didn't happen again. I never thought I had repressed much. I remembered too much. Everything.

"Look at what you have done, you fucking little asshole!" my dad would scream as he grabbed me by the scruff of the neck and threw me into the corner. "Stand there like that", he commanded as he sat in his chair, "Face the wall!". This was a regular occurrence. One minute, I would be playing in the lounge, putting the Monsters in my Pocket into the fireplace and on top of the heater like they were on a castle. I had become used to standing in that very corner on the same spot for hours and hours. I never knew how long it was, but I know Trevor had sat there and watched at least two films while I tried to balance on each leg so that the other had some momentary respite, as both began to cramp and hurt. I longed to speak out and beg to sit down, but knew deep down that this would just enrage my father more. My legs ached for hours after, throbbing as I lay in bed. I never gave in though. I felt a certain defiance. One day, I would outgrow all of this. I would survive it and endure. One day, I would get the upper hand. I guess this is where I differ from some abuse victims, I always knew it wasn't my fault. Nothing that happened was ever down to me. Who in their right mind would do such things, cause such destruction, and then when they are beaten, do it all again? I think deep down my dad knew exactly what was going on, as he never took me to a doctor to see if there was anything mentally wrong with me. He never took the time to check if I was actually all right. That told me everything I needed to know. This is why I could never respect him, because he knew what Alison did and he chose to ignore it, because he didn't want to be alone. Pure and simple. He was afraid of being alone.

When I wasn't stood in the corner, I was allowed to play with my toys in the lounge. I was never too far out of the line of his sight. My sister and I were sometimes allowed to play with my dad's fruit machine in the kitchen, but we had to play with our own pocket money, which we never got back. Throughout these brutal years of my life, I guess I learnt endurance, I would never admit defeat, I had been hardened at a young age. I always still had this sense that things would change, one day. I knew when I went to school that I wasn't like the other children, most of them had two parent families, birthday parties, lots of friends. I had a fraction of that. I guess, I remember being young and finishing school, I was maybe six or seven years old and my dad would forget to pick me up from the school gates, so I would walk the few miles home. Up and down the lanes, across the train track and then across the main road to get back to West Park. The times he did remember to pick me up, I would then spend the rest of the afternoon sat in the Redruth betting shop, drawing on the betting slips. My father was a gambling man, as I said before. He gambled his own mother's money away. He took advantage of people, borrowing or stealing money that he had no intention of paying back. He would have had a very nice home, good wife and a decent level of living if he didn't lose it all the time. My sister and I rarely got anything new from him. My mum would buy a lot of our clothes, shoes and school uniforms – my dad was very much in control of her still.

I would often sit upstairs and listen to my dad and Alison fight. I never knew what about, but I think he wanted her to leave her husband. She knew my dad was more interesting, but we all knew was that her husband had a lot more money. She also had a daughter called Vicky. I never knew if she was my dad's or not, but the thought often crossed my mind. Therefore, I frequently thought that Alison hated me and Laura, because her own child, who may have been my father's, had epilepsy, and she took it out on myself and Laura because we were fully abled children. Who knows what goes on in the mind of a psychopath? I knew that when my dad screamed at me and lost his temper, that Alison revelled in the damage she was causing. I had a reoccurring thought that there must be something wrong with her. Her soul was completely cold, devoid of humanity. When we spent time away from the clutches of Trevor and Alison, everything was so pleasant, fun and warm. I remember my mum walking me down to Portreath near the little bridge and the old tramline above. We would go to a little hairdresser down there to get my hair cut. I always remembered them playing songs that I was interested in and would listen to. Lots of Lisa Stansfield – I always wondered if she found her baby. I also recall Suzanne Vega, "Tom's Diner". Music was becoming a huge fascination and escape for me. I went from the love of my mother and my nan to the cold harshness of Alison upon the return home. She would usually look on as I took my 'punishments', with cold, glassy eyes. Occasionally she would chime in for Trevor to not hurt me, but not in a pleading way. More of a, maybe I have taken this too far, panicked sort of tone. Boy, did he beat me. I remember being beaten so fiercely once and screaming and crying so loudly, that the neighbour came knocking at the door asking if everything was all right. I was in agony, my hands stinging from being hit with the belt and slippers. The neighbour on the opposite side to Tim and Debbie was a policeman. Another piece of the puzzle where nothing was done to stop my father. He really could charm and fool everybody. They should have kicked the door in, called the police and had us taken away from him. It's a terrible thing to say, but I'd have taken adoption or going into care at that point. Everything was a horrible, terrible mess.

Daytime escapes were me going to school and then a lot of the rest of the time is hazy. A lot of it is probably repressed. I remember weekend days sat in the lounge with my father, watching his spaghetti westerns. He was a heavy smoker and I remember vividly the smoke hanging in the air, the rays of sun coming through the window breaking through the smoke. Sometimes he would play music and I recall seeing the video for Shakespeare's Sister, "Stay" and being really freaked out by it. I've since learnt that Siobhan Fahey was portraying death. It was her face that scared me and the whole scenario of being torn between two people. Life and death. This was my life at West Park from the ages of three to eight years. I knew no different. It was the life a child of that age should never have been living, but it happened, what else can you say?

Chapter 3

New Home

A new place to be,
Maybe a new hope.
Starving for freedom,
In a new home

1991 – 1, The Old Dairy, Plain an Gwarry

Moving to Plain an Gwarry felt like a new start, to begin with. I was a bit older and a little more aware. I went to the house before the people who lived there had moved out. I think the boy was called Tom. He had told me that strange things happened in the back bedroom. I have a memory of him living there and me being in that back bedroom with him and a shelf falling over. The first night I was going home to this place, I told my friends Hannah and Lucy that I would be walking home with them from now on and they didn't believe me until I showed them. We all lived in the same area. Redruth, it was off of the A30, down the hill past the Ambulance Station, you would then turn right opposite the Rugby club. This road led right through Plain an Gwarry, down to the brewery and then up from that was Redruth secondary school, with the lush green school fields. They were a series of large banks. There was an abandoned church on the right of the road, with broken stained-glass windows. It was fenced off and all boarded up, but we used to play there regardless. The launderette was right next to this and Lucy's house was the next house down. She had two huge fir trees in the garden and a pond we used to play with in the front garden. I remember as a child, that Lucy had pretended to have a twin who had drowned in the pond. The things children remember. There was a garage where we used to get all of our sweets, then there was the lane down to my house on the right, whilst directly opposite that on the other side was the Post Office. About ten doors down the road, towards the Brewery was Hannah's house at Canfield place. Sarah lived down the back of here, but eventually moved nearly opposite Hannah. Then there was Bruce, who lived opposite Hannah and next to the chip shop. Over the road again was another Andrew, my best friend in those early years. Down by the Brewery was Twilight Zone, the local club, and farther up the lane was a posh hotel called Penventon, or PV for short. The road led right through to the West End of Redruth up near the Fairfield. It was all pretty run down. There was a lot of disused, derelict land. If you came out of Plain an Gwarry and went right down towards the Portreath road and under the A30 viaduct, then you came to a huge, disused factory in a vast field with donkey rhubarb where we used to play and the old Fosters Pottery site. The area was massive and it seemed such a shame that it was all run down and abandoned, but it provided us with a huge adventure playground. Some of my favourite times and memories. At that time, the brewery was fully operational. I used to love the smell of all the beers being made and produced. West Park was right at the top of the Redruth School fields, so I had only moved a couple of miles away, if that. I lived in Plain an Gwarry from the age of eight until eleven years. Some of my most formative years. I had friends there. We used to play out together and go on missions and escape my awful life. We went on grand adventures to the beach, up to Carn Brea where I would always fall in a river. If anyone was going home with wet, squelchy feet, it was me. All of us children that lived there, were bonded together. I always had an odd feeling about the chapel up the road, I didn't like passing it on my own. I always felt or imagined that something might grab me in. I remember finding a shell in its grounds one day and when I took it home hundreds of earwigs kept coming out. It was disgusting. I learnt not to take things from sacred places then.

The house itself we had moved into had an odd feel about it, I didn't understand what it was at that age. I always felt that there was something in the dark, but I didn't know what. It wasn't the actual terror that frightened me, it was the unknown. I used to think I could see a huge spider web in the back airing cupboard, it almost vibrated there. I didn't understand. Years later I came to see this as energy of some sort. It was energy I could see with my own eyes. I guessed it was something bad as it made me feel frightened. I guess I just didn't understand, I was so used to being frightened most of the time that that was my go-to emotion.

There were some good times, when Laura and I were away from home with our mother, stepdad and extended family, it was like we were just normal children. We had a normal life, we did things that everyone else does; went on trips, holidays to the caravan at Kennack Sands. Funny memories, like forgetting the food bags and having to drive all the way back to Portreath for them. Another time, I remember my mum pretending to bop me with an umbrella and the extension bit popped out and hit me in the face. Just moments, when we could be funny and normal. That's how life should have been. I was too young to feel angry as I didn't really know any different. I didn't really know the enormity of my situation at that point, I had too much anxiety to be agitated with what they continued to put myself and my sister through.

Alison didn't cease her activities, she continued to do the same things, sometimes new things and it escalated. She would squirt the Fairy Liquid in the fridge when no-one was home. Sometimes, Laura and I would come back before our dad could discover it, we would madly clean it before he came home. The evil woman would still come into my bedroom at night and slap me or pull my hair. She would even steal our Christmas presents. One year, I knew I was getting a super soaker. This poor excuse for a woman stole it and destroyed it. My father went ballistic, accusing me of taking it out and losing it. I had to make up a story that I took it out to the park and some older kids stole it from me. She watched on as he beat me time and time and time again; hands, legs, feet, chest, anywhere he could. My hands were the favourite place for him to hit, and boy did it hurt. The more I cried the harder he hit me.

It was at this time, that I began to get into music more and more, escaping the reality I was in. I used to record the Top 40 on my cassette player and listen to it back, trying to get to the end of the song and press stop before the DJ spoke over it. My sister played her happy hardcore and I grew up listening to all of her music as well. I began to listen to songs like, "Linger", "Zombie" and "Dreams" by The Cranberries. One of the first songs I ever brought on cassette was, "Set you free" by N-Trance – a song that would follow me through my whole life. All the songs that were released around this time, Inner city, "Good Life", used to give me hip hop, dreamy vibes and I always wondered what it would be to have a good life. Soul to Soul, "Back to Life", was very similar for me. The escapism music provided for me was endless. Every song, every genre, I loved it. I went to discos with my sister and would hear songs like, "Blame it on the Boogie", "We Didn't Start the Fire", "Doctor beat". When I returned home, I would listen to radio ballads such as, "I don't want to lose you now" by Gloria Estefan. I didn't always know what the lyrics meant, but my tastes were very mature for my age. I loved other songs from the early 1990's such as, "Just be good to me", "Gypsy Woman", so many songs I look back on that provided the soundtrack to my life at the time. "Save the Best for Last", "Everybody's Free" and Roxette, "It Must Have Been Love" and "Joyride". I look back and see a theme of songs and music for the lost. Songs full of searching and yearning. I did enjoy fun music like, "Love Shack" and my friends and I would sing along to these songs with hairbrushes and pretend microphones. When we went to my mum's, she would listen to Michael Jackson and Simply Red.

I loved "Moneys too Tight to Mention" and "Something's got me Started". I had inherited my mum's love of music. There were just times I remember sitting behind the sofas at my mum's house in Portreath, with the headphones on and just listening to the music whilst reading John's National Geographic's. I was free and at peace there. The thought of returning to the lair of Trevor was distant in those moments.

We did mostly go without. It was only on the odd occasion when he had won some money on the horses, that we got something good. The one thing that Trevor brought for me and Laura, that was really for us, was a NES console. We had "Super Mario 3" on it, which I loved. I loved immersing myself in the make-believe world. We played "Bubble Bobble" and other games that we used to be able to play down at the local arcade, next to the cinema in town. Our dog, Sasha was of great comfort to me as well, she used to come and sit with me on the sofa and I would take her out for walks. The poor dog was treated cruelly by my father as well. As the abuse from Alison escalated, it resulted in her doing things that now cost a lot of money, like scratching the lenses of my glasses and breaking the arms off them so that they had to be sellotaped together. My father thought it was me acting out; scratching my glasses and carving pictures into my chest of drawers was extremely challenging behaviour for him. Of course, I never did any of them. Not one. Not once. Of course, I was ritualistically beaten for all of this. Sometimes Alison would be there to watch the carnage, other times she would set it up as a trap so that Trevor, Laura and I were all caught out by surprise. There weren't always dark moments, but I remember those a lot more than the good times. But there were good times. Not with him or her, but when I was with what I would call family and friends, when we were left to our own devices to do what we wanted. That was part of growing up. That was real. The only times I ever felt truly happy was when I was out with my friends. I know they must have thought something was going on at home, but it was like an unspoken secret. I didn't have the strength or inclination to tell anyone. It was just the life I was used to, no matter how unfavourable it was. That was my norm. I was in constant worry that if anyone knew, then we would be taken away and lost to the system, or worse he would kill us. I began to understand the enormity of going into care. I was becoming old enough to understand why he acted like this towards me and the degree of the violence showed his complete loss of control. I used to try and do things in advance to pacify him or stay out of the way whenever he was home. As a result, I spent a lot of time alone in my bedroom. I had games, a TV and music, so I was fine in there. I wouldn't know that some twenty-five years later I would be pretty much stuck inside with my TV, games and everything else, during a global pandemic.

Over these years, I bonded with my friends – we had such great times in the sun, in the rain, whatever the weather. We used to call for each there and if you didn't know where anyone was, you could tell whose house we were at by the bikes outside. I loved going to my friend Bruce's house to play with all his cool toys and his Sega Master System. I loved "Psycho Fox" and "Sonic the Hedgehog". His mum also owned a little pizza shop right at the back of the cinema, on the way into town and she used to give us free pizza. Her name was Mo, I assumed for Maureen, she was a very kind woman. These were the moments that defined my childhood. Just moments when we were all hanging out and none of our home lives or problems mattered. We collected our Mini Boglins and stickers. I collected my "Animals of Farthing Wood" stickers and magazines. The good thing about Trevor was that he pretty much left me and Laura, most days, to our own devices, so we would just go out all day with our friends, escape. If he was home, he was watching films on the TV and paying us no attention or he was in bed with his latest woman. We had the run of the area when we were out. We just enjoyed. That was our freedom. Meeting up with my friends and going on the school banks was always a good choice. There was a small woodland behind the local nightclub, Twilight Zone, and it sort of led up to the doctor's surgery at the edge of town. There was also a lot of abandoned buildings here that had burnt down in the late 1970's. We used to play in the woods, then march around an old well and through a field. We would then climb a huge wall to go on a mat swing we found at the learning disabilities centre. It was here that we also used to hide in the bushes and throw the little berries off plants at people as they went by, and then dart back into the bushes. We laughed, we played and lived our days away. We all had our own trauma, but when we were together, we felt unstoppable.

One evening, I arrived home from a bike ride out and playing "Please Mother May I" at the park, to my father seething. He asked where the Super Mario game had gone for the NES. I instantly knew she had taken it. I didn't know what to do or what to say. As he rained down blows on me, I cried out that I didn't know. He spat obscenities at me continuously until I made up a story that I had taken the game out with me and lost it. In a complete state of confusion and disarray, I then took my father out around the block, pretending that I may have lost the game over here, or over there. We never found the game. She even stole the "Green Jelly" tape that I had borrowed off of another friend called Terry. Terry barely ever forgave me for that, but how could I tell him Alison had stolen it and destroyed it on purpose like she did with the Super Mario game?

We never found anything that she took. Alison used to sneak into the house on a Wednesday night, when my father was out playing cards. That was when she would do her things. She even came in on me one night in the bath and pushed me under the water. She held me there until I could barely breathe and as I fought out, I spluttered and choked on the water. She never really spoke to me while doing any of this, it was always a silent attack like a predator stalking its prey. She was like a phantom looming out of the darkness. I could still taste the shampoo that had been in the bath water even after I finished my bath. The taste lingered in my mouth even after I brushed my teeth. Everything that she threw at me just became normal. I was quietly imploding but I was also developing a thick skin, as I had endured this for years at this point. She took every opportunity to try and hurt me. Not long after that, she began to effect my school life. I mean, it was already effected as I was constantly tired or feeling ill with worry. Mostly, school was another escape though, where they couldn't touch me. I would come home from my friends and would discover Alison had torn up my school reading books. Every time I went to school, I had to lie to my teachers and pretend that I had lost the books. This got me into trouble at school. She ripped the books up so often that at the age of nine I began to skive school. Not because I didn't want to be there, but because I was so worried about getting into trouble there as well as at home. I used to skive off anywhere I could. There were a couple of places in town where I would climb on a roof and stay there all day, singing songs to myself or just sleeping. There was also a disused building in the middle of the town and I would crawl in under a door there and lay on top of the rubble for the whole day. I would just sleep the time away. Sometimes I would hide down at the local park and older boys would find me and let me tag along with them to the Job Centre that was up past the park at the top of Claremont Road. I also used to scale the wall and tree here in search of conkers. I went to any place I could really. I grew up fast. I was caught one day, as I was seen at Victoria Park and the Head Teacher came and found me behind the bandstand with the school secretary. I did tell a passing member of the public that my name was the same as a local Chinese boy, so it was obvious what I was doing. A member of the public called the school. Why didn't they take more notice and work out what was going on? When Trevor found out about this, it was the cause of more beatings. Throughout all of this, there were happy times at Plain an Gwarry when I was spending more time out with my friends. Escaping. Or when I was at my mother's. However, it was all respite from what awaited me at home. I experienced things that no child should have had to. My sister and I grew up too fast and saw too much, we should have been children with no worries or cares in the world. We didn't have that kind of childhood. I know that I always wondered what I would be going home to and this constant worrying was an emotional drain on me. Looking back now, I wonder how I endured all the atrocities that Trevor and Alison inflicted upon me. It must have built up my defences and taught me to be strong. I was broken, but I was solid. It's always taught me one thing, that even though I may feel anxious or worried or not good enough, I have come through everything. I have endured. That is my act of defiance against those two and what they did to me. I continue to go on.

When I lived in this small street on the edge of Redruth, I'd socialise with my friends. They were my therapy and escape. I constantly repeat the word escape as that is what it was. I caught glimpses of what life should have been like. I never wanted to go home and Laura was the same. We would both try to stay out as much and for as long as we possibly could. Some days when Alison was there and being very controlling, I wasn't even allowed out of the doorstep and my friends weren't allowed in, so we had to have a quick conversation right there on the doorstep. I always wondered if my friends knew. People must have heard the sounds of me screaming and crying as Trevor lashed me again and again with his belt. It wasn't always bad. When he wasn't there and I was alone, I could do what I wanted to. I would listen to the radio or watch my television. Sometimes you had to press all the buttons in on the bottom of it and turn the metal handmade aerial to get a picture, but it was mine and I could watch it whenever I wanted to. Just down the road from where all of us kids lived, was the disused factory that backed onto the Brewery. The Brewery was extremely old and well known. We used to climb in through the back of the old factory and steal Piermont from the Brewery and sometimes cans. Then fall around as if we were pissed. We wasted a lot of the drink from spraying it around for fun. We played in the light areas of the factory, these were lit by the broken windows or holes in the roof. We never strayed into the darker areas, who knew what was lurking in there? I knew that homeless people sometimes stayed there and there were probably all sorts of drug addicts, maybe monsters, who could say? We had so much fun just playing around outside in the sun, exploring the local area, making a menace of ourselves. We would play in the park and spin off of the monkey bars, go as high as we would on the swings and burn ourselves on the hot slides under summer heat. The awful dropping feeling would be in my stomach every time I went home. The feeling was almost constant. It was either that or I would shut down to the point where I never felt anything. The ever-present knot would tighten in my stomach as I would approach the front door, concerned of what may be waiting for me. Most of the time Trevor wasn't even there, I had my own key, although the door was usually left unlocked anyway. There were occasions when Alison had stolen my key and I had to pretend to look for it around the house, until I was given a new one. One time I remember being locked out, so I walked in the rain and when I found an old trolley in a lane I pushed it under the steps of this big building and went to sleep in the trolley. Through these years and endless, long, lonely days, I would just sing songs to myself over and over again. That's why music was always so important to me. it was always a means of escapism.

Some of the things we did as children were so deadly and dangerous, like jumping from walls onto mattresses, setting huge fires and running along the roofs of abandoned buildings in the local town. We had no idea of consequence or responsibility, but these are all things that come with age. Sometimes I wonder if I was so reckless as it was like a freedom when I wasn't at home. I took bigger risks when I was out, because I had no power or control at home. Sometimes we did hurt ourselves, but we didn't say anything, we just went home and slept it off. I was used to pain, so hid any fun falls well. We taught ourselves how to look after each other and all grew so close. We learnt together. I admit, I probably didn't know how to behave sometimes and would act out, as this was the sort of behaviour I had learnt. I craved attention and any time it was given, I wanted more, so I probably came on to people quite strongly. Every day I learnt something, whether it be at school with the lessons from Mr Williams and then Mrs Probst. Miss Hard dragged me out of the classroom by my ear as I didn't have my books once again. These were the books that Alison had ripped up. I couldn't blame Miss Hard as she thought I was acting out as well. Every day at home, I learnt a lesson in how to look after myself, feed myself, or protect myself. It was nearly a weekly occasion that I would return home to find washing up liquid squirted inside the fridge. I began to develop OCD about this and clean incessantly whenever I found any, and whenever I thought that

I could smell it. I thought if my dad would catch a whiff of it, then he would beat me again. I was constantly grounded and my dad would say to me I would be ungrounded if I cleaned the whole house. One of these days of learning came when my friends and I, Hannah, Sarah, Andrew and Bruce had been in the local disused factory. We had run across the roof, through the next field, jump across the river and go into the old pottery. We found baby chicks stuck in glue as if they had fallen from a nest. We used to look around and collect the old plates and bits of pottery. I did have a vague memory of the place being open with the pottery all displayed and a pond inside, with big, orange fish. Everything was kind of chalky. The factory itself was huge and spanned three floors. We would act like immature fools and throw years old plates, which splintered sending shards of pottery in all directions. We tried to find a way upstairs, but the actual stairs had long since gone. There were huge rows of shelves that we could sit in and we began to climb on top in order to find a way upstairs. We played in here quite often, as the factory that stood next to the brewery ran down the side of the road and as you turned left and went up hill at the roundabout, there was the old pottery just before the school and the school fields. It was off limits and dangerous, but what else were we to do? There was very little in the way of activities and children's clubs around, there wasn't a youth centre, so we didn't have many places to go. My dad took myself and Laura out on very few trips, so we didn't do a lot – we made our own fun.

One day we were down at the old pottery and decided to do something we hadn't done before, "Wow, this is so cool" I said in awe, "Wicked", replied Hannah. "Cool..." added Sarah as we all stared around in awe at the floor to ceiling high paper files and perfect pots and cups still preserved in the abandoned pottery. A lot of local kids had previously been in the pottery, but this area seemed to be pretty much untouched. "Brilliant... where shall we make it?" enquired Bruce. "Right here", I said striking a match from the large box I pulled out of my trouser pocket. The box had obviously been easy to hide as the trousers I had on were quite baggy. I stole the matches from my dad's work stuff. He didn't really work, but I knew he claimed benefits and did some cash in hand jobs on the sly. Well, it was my dad after all, I expected nothing less. He had been in trouble with the benefits people as someone, I always hoped my mum, had reported him. I didn't expect him to work a nine to five or take me to school, or anything really. He didn't provide me with anything other than shelter. There were very few occasions that I remember him actually doing anything positive with me. It was always negative. He didn't want my sister and I at all, we were just two pawns in his game and control over my mum and my grandparents. The ultimate control. As long as he had us, he was still in full power over my mum, who had long since remarried and was happier with my stepdad John, than she ever was with him. Trevor was his own little dictator, forcing people to act certain ways and to respect him with a great fear. That wasn't real respect. Respect had to be earned. By having my sister and I, he controlled every member of our family. Who saw us, when they saw us and where they saw us. I knew if he found out I had stolen the matches, then there would be hell to pay. I remember thinking that if I was going to get a beating, then I may as well do something worthy of it.

As the little fire we made grew, Sarah and Hannah kept throwing small pieces of paper on that burned up quick and went floating up into the air. Little bits of ash floating about in the atmosphere like hot snow. There wasn't that much light in the room except for a few blasts of light coming through the boarded-up windows and, of course, the fire. I felt its warm glow against my hands. I often felt grateful when I was out of the house, just living in the moment and embracing the air, nature, and the momentary freedom. After a while, we got bored of the fire and decided it was time to put said fire out. We saw some wet, plastic sheeting that looked as if it had collected quite a lot of rainwater and tugged this over the fire. As the sheeting had a load of water in it, we all assumed that it would douse the fire and put it out, but instead of this it went terribly wrong. There was a whooshing sound and the plastic burned, releasing acrid fumes into the air. It grew out of hand very quickly. The flames licked upwards towards the ceiling as we stood there in shock and disbelief at what we had just done. "Let's get out of here!" I cried to Sarah as Hannah, disappeared down the hole we had all entered through. I went through the hole and as I went down, I lost my footing and fell to the floor with an almighty crunch. I lay there on the ground for a few seconds, motionless. Then the pain began to sneak in, my arms felt like they had been broken and my legs felt as if they had bent the opposite way. I had fallen on a half-broken pot and could feel the sharp shards digging deep into my side. I slowly, unsurely dragged myself to my feet, wincing in pain. I put my hand to the area on my side where the pot had hit. Looking at my fingers, I saw the wet blood that felt warm as it trickled down my side. The shards were very small, so they hadn't completely lacerated me, but they stuck in my skin like small daggers. Each piece was given a little tug to pull it out. "We need to get out now!" chanted Sarah, Hannah and Bruce together, "The ceiling!" I yelled. Just as we ran past the ceiling where we had been standing, it groaned and creaked. The area in which we had made the fire above began to buckle and turn black. The floor above us creaked again and sighed as it suddenly gave way, spreading flames and burning fury throughout the building. We exited as quickly as we could and ran to safety where we hid.

Twenty minutes later, we were these very naughty children, safely huddled in the donkey rhubarb plants between the old pottery and the factory. We often hid in there and built camps with the old discarded brewery crates. The crates were either dark red or green and had Redruth Brewery stamped on them, Established 1772. We all watched as the old pottery was surrounded by fire engines and police cars. I felt the twinges of pain as I plucked more of the pieces of broken pot out of my side, pulling on them as if they were tiny bramble spikes. We tried not to giggle as the situation soon turned to amusement. We had got away with it. This time at least. We had been lucky, as children usually are. Though on the way home, realising we all stank of smoke, I was covered in blood and dirt, and the others looked like they'd just come through a train wreck. It was at this point that I began to realise that danger wasn't just at home. If you put yourself into the wrong situation at the wrong time, the implications could be disastrous. However, for now, these memories guided me from my terrible home life through the trials and tribulations of what my father and his gruesome girlfriend could induce.

Whenever I was at home, I would mainly be alone in my room or my friends would come over. I had a bed on a slope over the stairs, so we could lay underneath my bed. We used to write all sorts of little messages, poems and general scribbles. We also used to do this in Hannah's airing cupboard, down the road. We would all lay on a shelf, sometimes sleep there for fun and just to hang out and chat. I remember the fun we would have creating our own radio stations and recording them with my cassette player. Role playing was a fun and social part of our lives. We all used to hang out and play computer games, all sitting back and watching while we waited for our turn. Most of the people we hung around with had a console, so I knew if I went to so and so's house that they had an N64, we had a NES, Bruce had a Master System. The other Andrew had the Mega Drive and I would often play "Columns," or we would go on long marches to the woods, the beach, anywhere we could find. We used to pinch my dad's tools to go to the local woods at the back of the doctor's surgery, near and old run-down building that used to be the pride of Redruth. There was a small section that we used to get in and we actually tidied it up, brought in some chairs and bits and bobs to make it like a den. I think a tramp started living there, as it wasn't long before it was boarded up and we were warned off by the local police. We would build treehouses so that we could hang out there and do whatever it is that kids do. In the woods was the old filled in well; we used to make little fires in there and share beer with anyone who had robbed it from the brewery. Sometimes, older kids would ask us to come and hold the fence while they snuck in to rob beer. They gave us some in reward. I loved the smell the brewery produced, even after living there for a while. We would meet at the park that was just around the corner. Occasionally, I would hear my dad whistle as if to call me home, that's when my stomach would drop. Every single time. Most times there wasn't anything bad, but sometimes, usually when you least expected it, it was awful.

So, those four years in Plain an Gwarry were filled with dread and fear from my home situation, but also a massive freedom and embracing of youth and young age. I had a lot of confidence when I was younger when I was away from home. I would try anything, do anything. I was probably reckless as I had been brought up with no boundaries. With this freedom came exploration, and there was a lot of exploring to be done. We would often take some sandwiches and a bottle of juice and disappear for the whole day. We would walk up to Carn Brea, which stood atop a huge hill and you could see to the sea pretty much in all directions. There were other outcrops dotted further up the county that you could see from here. There was a castle at one end, that was a sixteenth century hunting lodge and later left to ruin. What was so special about it is that it was built on top of the rocks. At the other end of the hill was a massive monument, some one hundred foot high built in the form of a cross, it was pledged to the Basset family who were a very highly revered family many years ago. Built with solid Cornish granite, it sat on top of the hill with other granite outcrops, formed thousands of years ago. Ancient. Wonderful. There were various rocks that we used to climb, such as Turtle Rock – I'm sure you can guess why the name. Elephant Rock, Foot Rock and so on. The giants head looking out to sea. There was also Sliding Rock, we would find old coal bags and use them to slide down this rock. The dangerous part was that there was a little rock at the bottom, so you had to try and dodge this in your coal sack otherwise you would get a big bit of rock up your ass. There were big bowl-shaped holes in many of the rocks that we used to sit in, these had obviously been eroded over thousands of years. As I said before, on the way there or home we would inevitably jump or come across the river or the Brewery leets and, of course, I would fall in or get wet somehow. I think it was because I was so small and just couldn't jump that far. The area of Redruth itself was pleasant and quiet, we never heard of much crime or anything like that. The local children were pretty free to do what they wanted, and we never really heard of anything terrible such as paedophiles or anything. Redruth was a plush, green area and was an old mining town, much of it long shut down. The old mine workings had fallen into ruin many years ago, but rich mining history was still there. The feel of the area was special. I always thought to myself that this was my home, whatever I went through. This was my home, my little bit of land to live in and no-one could take that away from me. I always said to myself that I'd rather be in Cornwall living alone, than living out of Cornwall with people that I didn't connect with. I felt a huge connection both physically and spiritually to the area. As with other things, it was a feeling I couldn't really describe or understand, I was just drawn. I was pretty sure by this point that at home, something was there. The energy I had mentioned before was always present. Nothing ever physically happened to me with regards to the energy, but I felt that something was still in the back bedroom and I often felt that if I went downstairs in the dark, that I would see something I didn't want to see. I didn't understand if I just was afraid of the dark, whether it was some sort of anxiety or there really was something there.

Time passed slowly, and I got very much more into music. I would go to John Oliver's to buy cassettes, then later, CD's . We used to earn money locally by knocking on people's doors and asking them if they wanted their cars cleaned. Occasionally, we had got the money, cleaned the side of the car facing the house then legged it. I remember getting chill blains, after days of putting my cold hands into the warm buckets of water, my hands would always get itchy. I used to listen to things like The Cranberries and Cotton Eyed Joe. With the song "Linger", we would sing, "Do you have two smelly fingers!". I was a kid, so loved things like Zig and Zag, "Them Girls" and all sorts. However, I began to love music like Lisa Loeb, "Stay", The Crash Test Dummies, and my go to song, "Set you Free". I used to listen to the remixes of that song over and over again, falling asleep to them. Musical stories, taking me away into the night. I had a varied and eclectic taste. As well as music, my other escape was my dreams. I would have night terrors and remember constantly calling out for my mum whenever I slept down there. At home, I was always too scared to leave my bedroom at night in case I came across Trevor or Alison. Not that that stopped her when she would decide to come into my bedroom and hit me about the face during the night. In dreams, I could be anyone, do anything. I would dream about amazing, vivid things like flying and being bathed in beautiful light. There were also the darker dreams. I would dream I was trapped, being chased by something, held down. It didn't seem to be the same fear about Trevor and Alison, this was another fear, like something else was after me, beckoning me somewhere that I didn't know. One of the scariest dreams I recall having, was being stuck in some sort of tunnel and trying to get out as quickly as I could. All I knew was that as I ran forward towards the end, the tunnel was getting smaller and smaller, darker and darker. I never made it to the end. The tunnel would suddenly shut and I would wake up gasping for breath. I would, in later time, learn that these were panic attacks and night terrors.

At school, we learnt all the normal things children should learn. I don't know how my teachers never saw my bruises or guessed what was going on at home. They must have known something. I didn't always behave like a normal child, I was very angry. Other times very quiet. I would sometimes hit out at other children and I just didn't know how to interact completely normally like everyone else. I either tried too hard or not enough. When we had sports day, I was really good at the sprints as I would imagine I was running away from everything. I was fast for someone so young. The teachers taught us about blessed gods and told us allegories of old. I enjoyed school as it was the escape I needed once Alison had stopped tearing up my books. Once I had been caught skiving at that age, I didn't do it again. I had been beaten within an inch of my life again. I was like a cat; I didn't know how many lives I had left. I have so many good memories of being young as well, they were sparsely intermittent, but I look back with a fond nostalgia for myself and my friends. The kids I grew up with in Plain an Gwarry. That was where I felt I belonged in a strange way. That was where I was meant to be. The memories become slightly misty and bright as years and time passed, but the feeling remains the same, there were moments when I was just free. The laughter. The warm rain. The sunsets and coming home late in the summer. Precious moments that take me back to some sort of primal fulfilment. My childhood should have been like that all the time. Unfortunately, it wasn't, so the highs felt even higher and the fear and lows were terrifying.

By the age of eleven, things at home had almost come to a head with Alison. The torment had become more wicked and twisted, with my dad coming up with ever worsening punishments. The beatings were frantic and constant. I would try not to cry or wince when he slapped his belt across my hands, but this would only make him do it more. Then I couldn't help but cry out, as it stung to the bone. When my dad returned home one evening, he discovered one of Alison's surprises, as she had a thing for creeping into the house on a Wednesday when he was guaranteed to be out, playing cards. She had poured turpentine all over the clothes in his chest of drawers and poured glue over his work tools in the back bedroom, that I was convinced was haunted. The turpentine had been in this storage room behind his bedroom and he automatically assumed that his son, me, had done this. I mean, who else would have done it? I had a history of this after all. Everything was absolutely ruined and in a weird, twisted way, I could understand why he was so angry, but it wasn't me. Trevor went absolutely ballistic, his face reddened with rage. He was like a man possessed and beat me for two days solid, so badly that I couldn't go to school. I could barely even sit down or put my hands down properly. I remember laying on my bed in my bedroom, trying to recover and waiting for him to come in and beat me again. In between the beatings, he ran into my room and hissed, "Eat this". It was a tomato. There was never a huge amount of food in the house and as I had already been beaten, I took a bite out of the tomato as if it was an apple. I immediately felt the tooth that had been wobbly, dislodge and come out. I didn't even attempt to take it out of my mouth, the tooth fairy would not be visiting me whatever happened. I swallowed that tooth instead. Like everything else, I swallowed it down and got on with it. That was my norm. That was my life. Social services had been called at various points over the years, but nothing ever happened. I recalled times at West Park when he had prompted my sister and I on what to say. It was very much the same scenario on their further visits, there was no rescue.

I lay in my bed huddled in agony, grimacing at every slight twitch or movement I made, wishing for the bruises to heal and the pain to end. I thought how evil and truly underhand someone would have to be or who could even do this to a child. It was at this point, Laura took me one day and we ran away to our mum's house. We walked all the way from Redruth, down the old Portreath Road, under the viaduct and then through the lanes. When Trevor learnt of this, he banged on mum and John's door to claim his children back. He punched John in the face and then withheld our visits for as long as he possibly, legally, could.

The time spent alone in my room grew, listening to the radio and playing games with myself. I was so used to this that I was very self-sufficient, I would often ride my bike around the area and go to the local woods down at Tehidy. It was just on the return home when that feeling would return and my stomach would drop, and I would wait and see what was at home awaiting me. It was a repetitive, common feeling. Every time, I thought it was so unfair that I should have to feel that way. I should have wanted to go home and tell my parent about my day, share things in a happy way. There was never any of that, it was a desolate and bleak environment to live in. One evening, I was watching television in my bedroom and Alison came in. She threw me off of my bed onto the floor and then grabbed the plate I had had a sandwich on, and threw it, smashing it over my head. She later told my dad that I had thrown this at her. If only he realised. At the time, I never thought he did, but deep down I do believe he knew. The pair of them were a step away from being serial killers like Fred and Rose West.

The viciousness of the punishments and the escalating frequency of the things Alison was doing, meant I never went a week without a beating. It was at this point in time when Laura was caught shoplifting and had stolen a lot of stuff, I couldn't blame her though. The role model we had, had us stealing things from supermarkets as soon as we could walk. It was all learnt behaviour and a cry for help. He even went as far as taking all of the stolen items off of Laura and gave them to us as Christmas presents. There was no length this man wouldn't go to, no depth to which he wouldn't stoop. I wondered why he didn't just give us to my mum if I was this much trouble, but deep down he knew it wasn't me and that was partly why my hatred for him simmered for so long – it was preventable.

We had lived in Plain an Gwarry for nearly four years and after a while, I learnt to love that house. There was something a bit off about it. The haunted back bedroom and the energy in the hallway cupboard, but still I was drawn there like I was happy to be there. Even though such terrible things went on behind the closed doors of 1, The Old Dairy, I still kind of felt that that's where I wanted to be. I lived with a small defiance in my mind that I would never turn out like my father. I knew his father had beaten him and I was determined to break the cycle of abuse. I didn't think it would be hard, as I never ever could be so brutal to anyone. Another day, Alison smashed the fish tank with my bike to make out like I had left my bike against it and that the dog had knocked it and cracked the glass. I came home to find all of the water pouring out, the fish were dead. It was another night I ended up beaten and sent to bed. I would sneak down in the night sometimes when I knew he had gone to bed, to eat cold beans straight out of the tin so that I could hide the empty tins deep down in the bin under everything else, so that he didn't know I had eaten anything and so that he wouldn't know I'd gotten out of bed. He had put a bolt on the outside of my bedroom door anyway, so whenever he wanted to, I could be locked in my room for hours. I was quite happy in there doing my own thing, I always found ways to occupy myself. I had little Kinder Egg toy collections and power balls and I built a big box out of straws to keep them all in. I was stealing a lot of things at this stage, I was like my father – if I saw something that I wanted, then I took it. In Year 5, I remember taking lots of plastic twenty pence pieces with Lucy and Hannah. We found that they worked in the twenty pence machines down at Sandy's Store and in town by the cinema. We stole all the toys out of them. There were power balls, trolls and all sorts of little treasures. I, however, was young so didn't understand the consequence of theft. The store owners realised it must have been a child and approached our school. We were caught and I was banned from going away on camp, that was my consequence. How did I get caught out so fast, yet my father got away with everything, year after year. I had learnt from my father though. It was all learnt behaviour. Even at that age, I had a slyness and want for anything that I could get my hands on, but I was definitely learning. Sometimes, I was locked in my room for so long and I became so desperate for the toilet, that I would have to wee into a cup or if there was nothing at all, it would have to be out the window or into a drawer. This was not normal behaviour. He would then beat me for this as well, even though he had caused it. The cycle was never ending and constant. At that age, the repetition seemed endless. I was so used to it that that was my life, there were brief moments when I was with my grandparents, my mum or my uncle Steven and auntie Julie when I was really happy, but I even stole from these people. I had an addiction, a behaviour I had learnt from my own dad, who should have been a role model. Instead I was a tool.

After another beating, I laid on my bed, hands throbbing with the belt and slipper stings and sides hurting where he had punched me. That night as I slept silently, my dreams flickered to a vision of a large Victorian house with a small topiary bush in the front garden, with a low granite wall. I moved inside of the wall and heard the gravel on the path as I walked towards the door. I entered and began running from room to room, looking for something, but I didn't know what I was looking for. The wallpaper hung gloomily on the walls and looked greyed with age from the brilliant white it had probably once been. There were different Greek scenes and faces on every part of the wallpaper and they stared out eerily. I was hunting for something, and I knew that when I found it, it would be worth it. I came to a taller door that seemed larger than the rest and stretched into a weird angle at the top, where it was painted in a dull, thick brown. That seemed very odd as all the other doors I had opened were white, except for the bathroom that had three glass panels that were frosted so you couldn't quite see through. I expected that if you put your face right against it, that you would be able to see the bathroom beyond. The house was pretty dark and I moved quickly down the hallways, looking. I wasn't even sure what I was after. I went back to the brown door and gently turned the handle, it was a round handle that gave a little click as I turned it. On the other side of the door lay a darkened room, the walls looked yellow and dirty... old. I pushed the handle and opened the door further, it squealed open. I saw them laying on a chair in the centre of the room. This sparked familiar memories of porcelain dolls and dolls that opened their eyes. The fear stemmed from very early childhood when my grandmother on my dad's side had died and left Laura a small Scottish man in a kilt and furry hat; every time you moved him, he opened his eyes. She also had a little mini Eiffel Tower, but that wasn't creepy in the slightest. Things like porcelain dolls and weird things that open and close their eyes, had always struck fear into me as a young boy and often filled my dreams with terrifying nightmares of moving dolls and glowing eyes. I thought of the X-files episode when the doll makes people kill themselves by telling them what to do. Unpleasant and vile. It made me recall a dream I used to have when I lived at 4 West Park about red eyes, glowing under the stairs and something coming out of the darkness to get me.

I wanted to back out of the room, but there was an invisible wall behind me. I was almost frozen in terror to the spot. The doll nearest me on the chair, turned its head and its eyes clicked open. The moonlight blazing in through the window was the source of fluorescence in the room and it shone brightly, showing all of the cracks in the porcelain dolls face. The doll next to it remained lifeless, but this one glared at me, longingly, yearning for me to come close so it could do unspeakable things to me. Rip me to pieces. I could feel my body beginning to push out beads of sweat, I held the doll's stare and moved towards the window, but accidently caught the corner of the table which knocked a shelf over, causing a few dolls to fall onto me that I hadn't even noticed. "Ahhhh…", I screamed as I threw them off of me. Had their tiny fingers just come to life and grabbed at me as they fell? I turned to look back at the doll to find it was gone. Panic flooded my body, I fled the room and pulled the door shut securely behind me. Something pulled back. Only once, but it was enough to shock me and for me to pull and grip tightly onto that handle, as if something was going to rip that handle straight out of my hand. My breath was heavy with adrenaline, I tried to keep completely mute as I listened to the sounds of the dolls rustling around in the room – then there was silence. My ears pricked. There was a sound from the opposite direction. I turned to see a pair of red eyes down the furthest end of the house, near the kitchen. I heard a giggle. It wasn't a child's giggle, it was like an ancient, deep, evil giggle. As I stared at the red eyes, my own eyes began to bulge. There were multiple sets of eyes appearing now and a chorus of maniacal giggling, I could hear the shuffling of feet. The darkness seemed to grow around me. I didn't move. I couldn't move. I was frozen to the floor as if glued to it. I wanted to flee, I moved my eyes around, but couldn't see anything in the growing darkness. The eyes grew closer in the dark, their deep, malevolent voices gleefully chattered as they approached in the dark. My head felt like it was going to explode, I couldn't even remember if I had taken a breath in the amount of time that I had been stood there. All I could feel was earth shattering and blinding terror.

In my mind, I knew I should be running, but I couldn't. There was no escape. I guess it was a complete mirror of what was happening in my waking life. The threat of fear. The gleeful giggling. The constant blind panic. Out of the changing darkness sprang a ventriloquist dummy. It was momentarily in view, then gone. These were my worst nightmare. I feared dolls, puppets, but these were the really old dummies – the ones from, I would say, Victorian times. They just looked sinister and they never had a pleasant voice. The worst of all nightmares. I pleaded with my unconscious self to wake up. I was half aware that I was dreaming, but my body was powerless to do anything to aid myself in waking up. The dummies continued towards me, eyes glowing brighter red in the semi darkness. The hallway becoming more illuminated by the red glow of those eyes approaching. Faster and faster they moved, but they weren't reaching me as quickly as I had imagined. It seemed to take an eternity, like the hallway was stretching and they were still coming. They were dragging out and savouring their moment. I couldn't see the ventriloquist dummy. No words clearly presented from them, as all I could hear were mumbles, gurgles and giggles. Scratchings and scrapings. I knew they were gleeful noises. I felt their hard fingers touch the bottom of my leg and suddenly they were all on me. The reds of their eyes meeting with mine, blinding me with the ruby hue. The hands shredded at my body, my flesh tore. My skin was peeled and pulled. The screams and echoes of their delight as they engulfed me, it felt like every ounce of my being was being stripped away from me. I was powerless to move. Trapped in a moment. An animal in tar. A snared hare. The more

I tried to move, the more they tore at me. I could hear the chunks of skin being removed from me. Blood soaked the floor and walls as the red light began to fade and the pure darkness returned. The evil shrieks of pleasure began to fade, leaving nothing but a wad of messy clothes and entrails.

1995

I jumped awake in my bed, pillow soaking wet from the nightmare I had been having. That house seemed oddly familiar. It was a dream though, so thoughts of it soon faded as I would become more worried about what I was waking up to. Would Trevor even be there? Was he asleep in his room or on the sofa? You just couldn't tell. It was a constant thought process of planning where to go and how to do it without waking up my dad. He never took me to school anyway, so I would go and call for Lucy and Hannah. It had been many years coming, but it was all coming to a head.

The final day of my physical torture came, it must have been mid-1995, when I was eleven years old. It was just a normal day, normal to me anyway. I arrived home from school to an empty house, even Laura wasn't in. She spent as much time out with her friends as she could, and who could blame her? She wanted to be a hairdresser, but the ever-controlling Trevor even had to be in charge of what Laura did, and he did not want that. He found endless pleasure in destroying his own children's lives. As usual, my father would be out gambling and drinking somewhere. He used his child benefit, that was meant for us, his own pension from the army and whatever cash in hand work I knew he did. He even had a hand in selling stolen items from burglaries his friends had carried out. Trevor wasn't stupid. He sold the items quickly, as he knew if they got caught burgling houses, then they would go to prison. If caught my dad would plead that he brought the items in good faith to sell on. He wasn't an imbecile. This is what made the punishments so horrible, because he knew. Deep down, I knew he knew what was going on with Alison. Maybe he got off on it. It was a thought I had internally for a long time. It reoccurred often. So why did he carry it on? Did he think here was something wrong with me? Or was there just something very wrong with him? I always settled for the latter. I felt he must have taken a sick pleasure in beating me, because it happened so much. There was never any remorse. A demon took over him, but it was a demon he was in complete control of. I was a very perceptive boy and I could see that every scheme and deal my dad made, was dodgy and wrong. I had the best teacher, didn't I? I was part of everything he had done. To his friends, Trevor was a shining example of a man. He had a family and he would help anyone. He made out to others that his ex-wife was a hysterical monster. He would help anyone, I say again except his own family. As far he was concerned, his two children, my sister and I, were a meal ticket to free benefits. My mum pretty much brought all our possessions, we didn't get much off of our dad as most of the time the money had been gambled away. I remember one Christmas he gave Laura and I a load of cash. It was less than twenty-four hours before he asked for it back, promising we would have it back soon. We never did get it back. I can only assume it was gambled away. How I hated sitting in that lounge with the old fashioned wall clock ticking in the background as he watched the horse racing, room filled with smoke.

This was a defining day. There had been a lot of awful horrible days. All the fear and the worry, the constant stomach aches that gripped me every single time I thought of going home or approaching the door. Even when I was at my mum's enjoying my freedom, if the phone would ring, I was sure it would be him every time telling her to bring us home that very minute. As I returned home this day, I felt something in the air, an electrical snap of excitement. I walked into the lounge and there she stood, grinning. Alison had come over again. I knew subconsciously she had done something. Every visit there was something more. In my shock, I inadvertently knocked over the table beside the sofa. The sofa itself looked like it had been slashed with a knife or something, there were gaping holes all across the bottom edges of the sofa and the chair, there was no way I was going to be able to cover this up. As the plant pots, ashtray and debris hit the floor, I noticed that the phone, which had also been knocked from the table, hadn't come off its base. I grabbed it and tried to pull it from the base, the wire waving frantically as I pulled on the handset. It was glued on. I looked up in complete disbelief. My eyes met with hers as she gave a dry, evil smirk. I looked back at the cut open sofa; I could see the insides of it like a hollowed-out whale. That's when the front door slammed with Trevor's entrance.

"Look what's happened here", gloated Alison, her eyes sparkling with demonic intent, "and it doesn't look like the dog's torn it. Someone's cut it", she said looking at me. I felt as if my life was moving in slow motion. "What the fuck!?", Trevor said as he looked down at the sofa, exposing its insides. "And the phone...", she replied in the most unconvincing tone possible. I knew what was coming. This was going to be big. I don't think I was quite prepared for what was going to happen. I had become so used to the belt and the slippers. The occasional punch. A lot of mental and emotional fear. This was worse. My own father began to pummel me like I was nothing. A bag folding in the wind. I felt the air leave my body. I felt the multiple crunches as he flew into the biggest rage I had ever seen. My brain frozen in terror. Her face smiling at me.

I had always known Alison was the purest evil, she worked as a bereavement counsellor, a good cover for someone so damned. The things she did to me and my sister were beyond cruel, her pleasure was in comparison to an evil monster in a horror film. I couldn't describe the sheer joy at what she was watching. Like him, there was no remorse. She would have happily stood there and witnessed as he beat me to death. Trevor had gone beyond losing his temper, he was frenzied. His face was so red with rage that I thought he might start squirting blood from his very pores. I almost detached from my body, this was a coping mechanism I had adopted so that I was barely present when these things happened. They just happened to my body. That wasn't me. I wasn't there. Trevor, whilst calling me every obscenity he could reel off, a little cunt and bastard, asshole, the list is endless, dragged me into the kitchen. I cried and tried to drop to the floor to get away, but Trevor just dragged me into the kitchen by my neck and clothing and threw me into the corner. I let out a small whimper as I scrunched to the floor with a dull thud. I trembled into submission. "Get up!" screamed Trevor at me, spit flying from his mouth like a rabid dog. I was resigned to my fate. I knew there was nothing I could do, no way to fight back, so I stood up, shaking.

My father grabbed me roughly and pushed me towards the work surface, where he pulled a large wooden mallet from the drawer. For a second, I thought, at least it isn't the knife. He had always told me never to touch the knife, but I sometimes played with it when he wasn't home, chopping the wooden hammer into bits. My friend, Andrew had once hit the wooden mallet so hard with the knife that he cut his own hand – that was a lot of blood. Trevor gripped the wooden mallet, "Now tell me the fucking truth, you little bastard, what have you done?" he hissed, lining his eyes up with my poor, frightened child's eyes. "I didn't do anything", I sobbed. Smack! Trevor laid a blow across the back of my legs. As his hand connected it left a red mark on my legs, I winced in pain but stood firm. "I don't fucking believe you, hold out your hand", he commanded. I didn't want to hold my hand out, for I knew what would happen. I stared at the wooden mallet and looked at the deep cuts in it, remembering my friends and I chopping it with knives. I remembered how my own flesh and blood would force me to put my hand on the chopping board and threaten to cut my hands off with the huge blade he kept in the same drawer as the mallet.

"He's just a boy", called out Alison in an almost human tone, though her acting wasn't good enough. "Just stay out of this, you fucking bitch", snarled Trevor, "I will deal with this little bastard". My father grabbed my arm and thrust it onto the chopping board, holding it in place whilst he spat out the words, "FUCKING TRUTH, NOW!". "I don't know", I sobbed. All I could do was close my eyes and accept whatever card was going to be dealt to me now. "Put your fingers out flat!" he spat into my face, I didn't want to, I screwed my hand up into a ball. Alison watched on, her eyes shiny with desire and quiet rage that Trevor had dared speak to her in such a tone. She would make him pay for that later. Her cruelty knew no bounds. He forced my fingers open and pushed his clenched fist onto the top of my hand so that I couldn't fold my fingers back up. An adult's hand pushing onto the back of eleven-year olds, causing so much pain. I felt the breeze of the mallet go through the air as he rained a blow down on my thumb. The pain was sudden and went right up my spine and into my brain. I screamed in absolute torture, beyond anything I had felt before. I didn't want to look down. Surely my finger was flattened and broken. Surely there would be blood and gore hanging out everywhere. It felt hot and it throbbed. Trevor kicked me into the corner and then slide his belt from his trousers in one motion and set about walloping me constantly for ten minutes, lash after lash.

Suddenly Laura burst into the room, she had heard the commotion from the street as she came home and ran in. She flew in the door, hysterical with anguish and terror. Alison dodged around her like a ghost and swiftly left the house. She never stayed any longer than she had to, Alison just wanted to witness the damage she had caused and then go back to her other life, satisfied by the injustices she had dealt out.

"It was Alison!" Laura screamed as she tried to pull Trevor off of me. He hit out at her with his belt as well. Laura had been having her own problems and fucking up in her own way – I never knew any of this until years later, I guess we were just both stuck in our own constant fear and misery, caused by these two evil-doers. Everything these dysfunctional adults did, had taken over our whole lives like a disease. "It was fucking her...", Laura continued. "What?" said Trevor, confused, "I don't think... what?", he looked around for Alison in disbelief. He realised she had made a hasty retreat and gone home. Trevor turned back to me, full of devilish anger and severe lack of control, "Children like you, need to go to a special school" he paused briefly, "from now on, you will call me sir, won't you?". "Yes", I replied submissively as a loud swishing motion of Trevor's leg met with his very own son's stomach. "What did I just say, you fucking little cunt, what did I say to call me, you fucking piece of shit? It's yes, sir", he growled, pulling me towards him.

Laura was pulling at him to stop beating me and I don't really remember what else happened that day. I had been so badly beaten that I think I just blacked out from the persistent pain. All I do know, is that was the last day that anything like that happened. I do not recall Alison pouring bleach on clothes or turpentine in my dad's drawers again. There was no more washing up liquid squirted in the fridge or toys and games going missing. There was no more waking up in the night to being slapped or having my hair pulled. There was no more being hit with a belt and a slipper or being forced to hold my hands out as they stung in pain. I was eleven years old and had endured so much for someone so young. If only the people around me knew what I had been through. If only the people at school knew what was going on. I always knew this wasn't my fault so I guess that helped me, I was the victim. This was just something that happened to me. If I had known at the time that there were kids like me all over the country, all over the world that suffered like I did, then I wouldn't have felt so desperately alone. I'd never have been so afraid. All I knew was that it had to get better. Trevor collapsed onto the sofa and drank his bottle of vodka.

I sat up in bed, there was a strange smell in the air. It was like a musty, flowery smell. It reminded me of flowers that had passed their best and were wilting in the algae ridden water that held them. I knew that scent. I had a severely dry mouth. I decided to get up and get a drink of water. There was no pain from the earlier battering I had taken. Something didn't quite feel right, it was almost as if I was trapped in a fairground mirror, something was distorted even though it seemed fairly normal. It was very strange that I should wake up in bed after being so severely thrashed. I threw back the musty stained quilt, put both feet onto the sticky wooden floor and stood up. The smell made me want to wretch as it was penetrating my nostrils and lungs, it was so strong that it hung thick in the air. I always got a feeling when something wasn't right, I never knew what it was, but it was like an instinct. As I walked down the hallway, I was in the strange

Victorian house again. I walked outside into the back garden and saw a rose bush. The green garden blurry with the sunlight, I couldn't make out any other details. However, this didn't alarm me, I just moved through the grass, to the back wall of the garden and looked back. I looked back towards the back of the house, was that a flash of a face I saw in the upstairs window? I was back in my own house, in front of the sink. The tap divulged water with which I washed my face and drank from my hands. It was as dark as before.

I didn't want to end such a huge chapter of my life negatively, so felt the urge to talk about my loves of that time. Music and just hanging out with my friends. Those were the best of times. When I was carefree. When I embraced childhood and what it meant to grow, learn and just be with others. Children, or people who were the same. That is what it should have been like consistently. When I recount what my father and Alison had put me through, I can only feel sorry for that little boy I see in photographs, because I remember how much fear he felt and the anguish and pain. I see his face now and recollect everything he went through. I know he was a strong, brave, little boy who just got on with things. I see him now and I am proud that he held on, that he fought and that he won. I cannot thank and explain how much all my friends and family outside of Trevor, all did for me. If I hadn't have had them then, then who knows where I would be? We used to go to Hannah's house and I have a very vivid memory of her and her sisters, all dressing me in random girly clothes and dangling me from the window. We would run off out of each other's houses, down to the brewery leets to play. We had a little swing across one part where there was a big drain going underground, under the field. I leant over one day and the lenses fell out of my glasses. It was always a little reminder of something Alison had done, broken or destroyed. Another time, one of our friends swung across the river and the rope broke. He crashed into the river with a big splash . There must have been a broken bottle or something in there, as when he resurfaced, he had cut his head open. Blood flowed as fast as the river. It looked a lot more than it was, but there was a lot of blood. I recall a similar incident down at the local beach, we were jumping off the harbour wall and he happened to slice his leg on an oil drum. I recollect seeing the inside of his leg and feeling ill – it was a perfect slice, like a hot knife in butter. When we weren't injuring ourselves, we were just hanging around down at the park, down at the woods. We would scrump apples from trees. We were just normal children. There was no intent in what we did, we were just being free. It couldn't last forever.

The music I lost myself in around this time, gave me a fulfilling feeling deep inside. It stemmed a flow of thoughts about negative things and gave me some hope. Inside my room was a constant stream of different music, all genres, all types. I immersed myself in it fully. Music gave me a huge positive lift in the darkness of my life, it was there for me when I had absolutely nothing else. It transported me to another plane of existence. So much music. So little time. I was hungry for it.

I listened to music like people would read books. It had and still holds such importance to me. Snap, "Rhythm is a dancer", "Welcome to Tomorrow",

Haddaway, "What is Love?" engaged me in early dance music. There was so much to feed me, so many songs. Culture Beat, "Mr Vain", 2 Unlimited, "No limit", Urban Cookie Collective, "The Key, The Secret", Sub Sub, "No Love, No Use", KWS, "Please Don't Go" Inner Circle, "Sweat, A la la la la long". One song that particularly touched me, and continued to for many years without fail, was 4 Non Blondes, "What's Up?". I can't explain what the song meant to me, but it always elevated my mood. It gave me some sort of hope. Thoughts towards the future. There was also a rave remix, which I also recorded from the radio, DJ Miko, "What's up?". All the songs I could find, I wanted. I couldn't afford to buy them all, so I had to sit waiting for the Top 40 every Sunday and hit that record button over and over again. I listened to thoughtful songs such as Tony Braxton, "Breathe Again", Sophie B Hawkins, "Right Beside You", "Damn, I Wish I Was Your Lover" and "As I lay Me Down to Sleep", Meat Loaf, "Rock and Roll Dreams Come True". I loved songs like Neneh Cherry, "7 seconds" and Enigma, "Return to Innocence". If I was able to buy all of the music that I wanted, then my bedroom would have just been rammed. There was no end to the number of songs out there. I was very confident in my choices of music and I would play the songs over and over and over and over again. I must have lost countless hours just repeating all of these songs. Sometimes I would record one song, then wait for it to come on another day or another time and record it again so I would get like an extended remix that meant I didn't have to rewind as much. Tapes got chewed up very easily back then. I loved deep and meaningful music like Counting Crows,

"Mr. Jones", "Round Here" and Louis Armstrong, "We have all the Time in the World". We used to try and impersonate his deep, husky voice and sing like him. It hurt your throat. Still I respected and loved his musical creations even at such a young age.

Sometimes I would sit on the school fields with my friends, sharing a headphone or we had some plug in speakers. They were very small and rubbish, but for the time they were amazing. I used to take them in the bath with me. I loved dancing around to house and dance music when my dad wasn't there. My friends and I always sang along and danced to amazing tunes like Alex Party, "Don't Give me Your Life", JX, "There's Nothing I Won't Do", Grace, "Not over yet", Corona, "Rhythm of the Night", The Nightcrawlers, "Push the Feeling On", Whigfield, "Saturday Night". "Another Day", Pat O Banton, "Baby, come Back". The earliest Now I had was Now 29, with such hits like Michelle Gayle, "Sweetness", The Real McCoy, "Another Night". I pinched my sister's Baby D, "Let Me Be your Fantasy" cassette to listen to when she wasn't home, and I enjoyed it immensely. There was a song by a group called Snap, "Welcome to Tomorrow", I feel like I clicked with that song as I was always looking for tomorrow, and there was something quite magical about the song and the way it resonated with me. It was one of those songs that I forgot down the years, and I recall reaching back into my mind to try and remember it. When I did, it brought everything back.

I would dream myself into other worlds, places, anywhere else. These were creations that brought light to my life. I imagined myself in alternate dimensions. I dreamed sweeter dreams at times as well. When I was self-healing, I was also growing and learning. Music was my constant escape. If I was ever alone, I remember just playing songs over and over again. I look back now and think that music has a healing quality to it. I needed full healing and was eager for any input it could give. Music had such a calming effect on me. I loved Annie Lenox, "No More I Love You's", Tori Amos, "Cornflake Girl". I listened to my sister's happy hardcore music as well. She used to listen to Snoop Doggy Dog, "What's My Name", Cypress Hill, "Insane in the Brain" and "Ain't Going out Like That", The Prodigy, "No Good for Me" and Opus III, "It's A Fine Day." She also played Hip Hop that I didn't really understand then, but most of it was pure filth – K7, "Come baby Come". We just sang it and had no real perception of what the lyrics meant. Like me, Laura also loved music. Even though we were very similar, we were also very different. I think as Laura was older, she responded to everything differently to me. She remembered a lot more detail than me about certain events. We fought like brother and sister at a time when we should have been more bonded. We were lucky to have not turned on each other under such pressures. Things weren't always as dark as they had been. There was light at the end of the tunnel. Deep down I always had a glimmer of hope that things would be right one day. Things take time after all.

Chapter 4

New dreams and Growth

New dreams and growth,
It's in the distance, it's remote,
What you get, what you have heard,
Isn't what you need, or deserve

1995 – 138 Agar Road

We didn't live in Plain and Gwarry for long after that, we moved just as I was starting secondary school. Year 7, I had moved away from my friends. It wasn't far, but it was still a good forty-minute walk or a twenty-minute bike ride. I don't even remember moving to Agar Road. Trevor did it one day whilst I was at school and I went home to the new address. As I arrived, I noticed it was a big, tall Victorian looking house. Strange. Familiar. The gravel cracked underneath my feet as I walked up the path and approached the house. 138 Agar Road in Pool. The second I walked into the house, I knew there was something wrong. I couldn't quite fathom it, but as I looked up towards the tree and the sun shone brightly through a break in the green leaves I thought to myself, "I don't like it here".

I stepped over the threshold and my stomach felt knotted and my breath stolen. It was such an odd feeling. The house itself had a rather nice façade, it was a tall, Victorian building made with Cornish granite. It stood on a long road of old houses that dated back hundreds of years with its history deeply rooted in the mining industry. My father had once been a miner, but as with all of his jobs, none lasted very long. That path that led up to the house was made of pebbles, encapsulated with some type of mini log fencing. There was a large red gate to the right-hand side as you looked at the house, which gave access to the back entrance and yard. There was a very odd feeling about this place, something very perplexing indeed. I had never experienced a feeling like it. Like someone had sucked all of the air out of the room. The lounge was piled high with boxes, a Victorian fireplace stood grandly in the room, with a high ceiling and ornate coving.

I moved out into the hallway, flowing with the house. I turned right again into the next room. I noticed that the light switches for downstairs were on a panel outside of the room, situated in the hallway. I thought how strange this was – even in the daylight, something didn't seem right. It just felt dark and subdued. I didn't like change anyway, so that probably didn't help. The house itself, was huge compared to where we lived before, but still it felt empty and melancholy. I went through the back, into the kitchen and peered through the window. There was a long garden with a large shed situated at one side. It had a corrugated roof, which I imagined sounded really tuneful when heavy rain pelted down on it. I went outside into the shed and noticed how smelly and damp it seemed here as well. The shed was very big and there was my dad's old chest freezer plonked in the middle of it. The windows inside were very dirty and a brown muggy light penetrated, casting ugly shadows on the wall beside me. I noticed on the back wall were some pictures. They appeared to be random pictures of people smiling, in various scenes and also less happy faces. They looked Victorian to me, dressed in very smart clothing, some with very serious, almost dark expressions. I traced my fingers across them, brushing off some of the dirt. My fingerprints imprinted onto the old pictures. Something darted behind me, I turned around so fast that I almost got a head spin. There was nothing there. The shed door blew gently in the wind. I thought that it must have been that swinging in the breeze that caught my eye. I could see straight up to the main gate that led to the front of the house and could see my dad moving things from the car. I looked up and saw another tree above, lining the side of the house. It was possibly that moving and causing changes in the light and shadows, I thought to myself after the door gusting closed. The windows were very dirty and the light was filtered through, so it could have been anything really. Even a bird flying by. There were some pictures of horses and some other horse related items. I didn't know what they were, there was also a horseshoe. I think that was meant to mean good luck. Laura brought my bike into the shed and she turned around and put it down out of the way. At this stage, Laura had got a job at Safeway which was a minutes' walk from home, and she was steadily escaping. She had the means to make her freedom, something I wasn't yet ready or prepared for. Things at home were getting better, but

Trevor still tried to control both of us. Now Laura was working, she would have money. This would cause tensions as he would want some of that money, if not all of it.

Being a child and full of curiosity, I hopped out of the shed on the turn of a penny and decided to set up my new bedroom. Whether I liked it or not this was now home. I took myself upstairs to my bedroom and began to sift through my belongings; hanging clothes in the dark wardrobe and putting objects and half broken toys on shelves. As I did this, I had an overwhelming feeling that someone was watching me. My back was to the door and for some reason I did not want to turn around. I stood on the spot holding a T-shirt I'd just neatly folded, frozen for a few seconds until the feeling passed. It happened often, these strange feelings, but they always passed. Nothing bad ever happened, so I dismissed them as fear and tricks of the mind. When I was about ten, we did a Ouija board in the toilets at Trewirgie school as we thought a student had died in there. One girl said the taps turned themselves on and another said something threw some soap. I never saw any of it, and I am not sure if I made the Ouija board move or someone else did, but we carried it out either way. I do recall burning or tearing up the bits of paper. We used to sit in the corner of the playground and tell ghost stories and play other games.

Anyway, until you see something with your own eyes, it's hard to believe. It is very easy to dismiss something that you haven't seen or even believe in. On many occasions, I had a sense and a tingle down my spine and had spun around on the spot, to see nothing in the hallway behind me. "I must be losing my mind", I said to myself.

Trevor was downstairs unpacking things, Laura had gone out with some friends as per usual. The house was silent. My first night in the house provided me with a formative experience that never left my brain. I was made anxious by the new creaks and groans of the house, as it settled from the heat of the day to the cool of the night. I imagined it was the door creaking downstairs in the room I hadn't liked, and all sorts of weird and fantastical creatures emerging to take me away. I had always slept with the cover far enough above my head to let air in, but to keep anything from sight. I had done this for many years, since I was a very small boy. The warmth enveloped me nightly and provided comfort. Emptying my mind of all thoughts, I closed my eyes and breathed in deeply. This was a sort of ritual for me as it helped me in getting to sleep and not thinking about the awful things that had happened to me at the hands of Alison and Trevor in the past. These things I knew would never be forgotten and were so raw and painful – if only I knew then that time would heal all wounds. I focused on gently breathing in and out until I drifted off into a deep sleep.

The beatings had come to a standstill, all except for one moment when Trevor couldn't find a puncture repair kit for my bike and punched me in the stomach. That was the only physical contact he made with me again. He remained ever controlling of Laura and me. I think Alison would visit when we weren't there, but there was no sign of any wrong doings. I still checked the fridge and cupboards in case she had done anything. I was obsessed with checking and looking around the house just in case she had done something. I never found anything but the anxiety was constantly there. My father paid me to clean the house, so I earnt my pocket money. This would involve picking up dog poo, doing washing, hoovering, dusting, walking the dog, going shopping; everything.

I had a lot more room in this house. There was a decent sized bedroom upstairs and a room downstairs behind the lounge, that I made into a second bedroom. It was semi playroom, but I was oddly attracted to the room. It was also the room I didn't particularly like. A very contradicting feeling. I would spend a lot of time in there, recording songs off the radio or playing my new cassettes I had brought on my many cycles into town. It was huge compared to my old bedroom at the Old Dairy. I had a basketball hoop out the back by the shed that I played with. I had more freedom now, but I had more alone time as well, as my friends didn't live on my doorstep. I made other friends though and went out on my bike with them. I'd still go into town and find out what was in the charts, and buy all my books, magazines and more cassettes, stop at the shops and buy stickers for the various albums I had, and other little collections. I would line all of my tapes and little collections up in my bedroom. It was around this time, I became more aware of the presence of what I assumed were spirits or ghosts or whatever in that place. The house on Agar Road was haunted. I had avoided the thoughts for a long time. I didn't like it and I couldn't explain why, something just didn't feel right. As soon as I stood over the threshold, I knew it wasn't right. Just knew it. I always came back to that thought that I knew something was there. There was a darkness like a cloud enveloping the home. I spent a lot of time there, so got used to the way the house felt in the two years we resided there, a lot of it alone. I always felt as if there was an eye looking at me through the crack in the door. This happened all the time. It was like the anxiety had changed from the fear of beatings to the fear of ghosts or spirits, whatever they are called. That intense kind of pressure. I was doing well in school, living as normal a life as I could, probably processing the events of the past years.

I hid all my pain and anguish with jovial smiles, although I was in a state of constant anxiety. When I look back on it, I must have been suffering some sort of post-traumatic stress disorder. My behaviour was quite obsessive and I often got angry and tried to control other people I knew, friends at school. I almost felt like I had Asperger's Syndrome, as I wanted to interact, but I didn't quite know how to do it properly – everyone just thought I was a bit weird. I would still awake to find myself in the dark and full of fear, I learnt that I was having night terrors. They increased while I lived in Agar Road. I felt as if I was coming to realise something about myself, but I couldn't quite fathom it yet. I wasn't ready for the answer as to what it was. I felt that the house was haunted. I was obsessed with reading Point Horror, Goosebumps and ghost books. I also watched paranormal shows, like Strange but True and The X Files. DJ Dado had released a house version of the X Files theme tune, which I loved. It had a 'paranormal' remix on the other side of the cassette.

However, I didn't really know what a ghost or spirit was. I knew something was there, I felt its aura and I sensed its presence, but I couldn't have ever said what it was, whom it was or where exactly it was. I just knew it was there, present. The nightmares were as terrifying as ever. The daytime threat of the beatings and visits from Alison were fading. The wounds and pain still very fresh in mind. The house was like a dream I had had a few times. The Victorian building. The wallpaper. Like most things in my life, I never really questioned it, I just accepted things for what they were. I had lived for a couple of years in a very similar house called Erica, down the road. Maybe I remembered the layout from there or something. It was strange, but I had no answer. Every nightmare I had was the same, I would wake up in the dark and my eyes would not adjust. It felt like the blackness enveloped my body. There was a bright orange streetlamp outside my upstairs bedroom window. The downstairs room had thick curtains and was situated at the back of the house, so it was very dark. I was always in this room.

The blackness was dense, and I had to make conscious effort to move through it. I always felt like there was a presence behind me. Or it would be somewhere in the house, searching for me. I was always frozen in terror. I couldn't breathe and my lungs burned to scream out. I never did, I just recall the absolute terror. I can't explain how I knew there was a presence, I just knew. These kinds of occurrences were gradually becoming more and more regular. I knew things before they happened. Simple things that other people may say, I would say it just before them or I would think it and not say it.

As I lay in the darkness this time, paralysed, I thought how strange it was that I'd be in this sort of place. Something released me, and I got up and out of bed. I didn't search for a light, I just stood up and moved towards the door. "Shhhhhh", rasped something in my ear. I flinched and turned around in the darkness. I wanted to turn and flee, but I couldn't. It was as if my feet were stuck to the floor with glue.

Something gently tickled the back of my neck, as light as a feather, as a sickly fragrance began to fill the air. I thought fragrance, as it wasn't the usual stench of sewage or rubbish. This was like someone was overusing perfume to a serious extreme. It was a wrenching odour that made me want to wretch and gag. Out of the darkness stepped a shape, that I took to be Alison. The fear I had experienced for so many years grew again. The silhouette morphed into a different shape, it became more elongated and somehow in the darkness, it became darker. My eyes struggled to adjust, there was no light. It was a strange eerie illumination. Out of the darkness, it turned to me, head lop sided and humming an unearthly tune. Its eyes, slightly sunken into its white flesh. I had images of it sitting at a table with a mirror, preening itself like an unearthly jezebel, hair coming out in clumps with the brush. Pulled straight from the scalp. A kind of banshee figure that was coming to signal my death. Whatever this was, it felt truly evil. I had experienced real evil before, but this felt different. It felt as if it was looking into my soul, into my bones and it wanted to crunch them all.

"Why do you go on?" a rank, ancient voice croaked from its open mouth. I could see the bleeding gums and razor-sharp teeth that filled this non-human mouth. Its head hung oddly in the dark, at almost a ninety-degree angle. The teeth looked ripe for tearing flesh.

"We come from the dark places....", the voice trailed off as I remained frozen in horror. "We pity savaged souls", it continued, "We.... will show you". I was completely rigid. I wasn't processing anything, I just tingled with sheer horror. Whatever this was edging towards me, I couldn't move from the spot. I was suddenly in the hallway of Agar Road – I recognised the wallpaper. Behind me was the front door and the faint glow of the orange streetlamp dimly illuminated the hallway. The shape continued up the hallway towards me. I heard a gurgling kind of laughter, I squeezed my eyes shut and hoped that it would stop. It didn't. I felt totally sick. There was a huge anticipation within me. If I could have bolted, I would have, but as per usual, I was powerless. I was unable, I wasn't strong enough to get away. I saw a gaping hole now, where the mouth should have been. I investigated the blackness and saw the edges of the teeth as the orange light reflected off of them. I wondered where Laura and my father were whilst all of this was going on.

The gurgling and belching increased, it was as if it was saying something to me, but I couldn't understand it. I was too fearful to even attempt to know what it may be saying. It may have been saying nothing. Multiple thoughts screamed through my mind at once. Festering bodily fluids poured from the hole in its mouth, as it got closer and closer to me. I remember reaching out behind me, hand against the wallpaper, as if I could somehow pull myself away. I remember feeling the ridges of the wallpaper beneath my fingertips. The texture of it, soft but firm, almost spongy. "Sweet dreams", it hissed as it pounced, moving quicker than the eye could see. Swift and elegant like a black cat, the dancing shadows taking off my head in one swoop, leaving nothing but a spurting stump and a sickening crack hanging in the limp air.

I woke up with a start, drenched in sweat. This had become such a normal occurrence now, even after the abuse had ceased. Scars take a long time to heal, don't they? There was still always the nagging feeling that if I did anything wrong, then my father would lash out. I guess I was getting older and would soon be old enough to stand up for myself. This dream reoccurred often, but it was only when I was in that house. The fear felt as fresh as ever though, every single time I experienced the dream. The heart stopping, blinding terror. If I woke up at night and had to go to the toilet or something, I would often keep my eyes shut and feel my way around the house, as I had this awful feeling that if I opened my eyes in the darkness, I would see something – I didn't know what, but I thought I would see it and freak out. I was downstairs in my new home, in darkness. The orange hue of the streetlamp out front stumbled through the front door glass, which provided some light. My hand touching the end of the banister at the bottom of the stairs, moving into the kitchen, I felt my way along the work surfaces. The tap dripped, making a tinny noise as it hit the metal sink below. I found the light switch and turned the light on. My eyes were always drawn out into the dark garden and the shed. I always remembered the pictures that had been there and the eyes that had burnt into me. I thought it weird that someone would leave their horse items, ribbons and pictures there as they were like little memories or treasures. Leaving the kitchen and turning the light back off, I noticed the moon had come out which provided an eerie light when mixed with the streetlamp. The room that attached to the kitchen and the hallway before the stairs, was a strange little room, it didn't get much light and was very dank. It had a little fireplace, but it just felt off. The room just beyond it as well. This felt like the focal point of the problem I thought, the area where the coldness started. Maybe something awful had happened there. As I approached the edge of the stairs by the light switches downstairs, I heard a scuffling in the room behind the lounge.

There was a definite noise now, it sounded like a mouse scuttling around inside a box or something, scratching to get out. I didn't feel scared, but was aware that the hairs on my neck were standing up. I made a grab for the light switches and flicked them all on, so light illuminated the hallway, lounge, dining room and the black room behind the lounge. I never usually turned the lights on, in case Trevor woke up and shouted at me for being out of bed. He was normally too drunk or passed out on the sofa, with the door shut anyway, so he was out of the way. Thud! I froze in fear. I stood bathed in beautiful light; it should have made me feel safe, but it didn't. My body went cold. I could still hear the scuffling sound, so went towards the door and turned the handle. The door swung open in front of me and I started to walk in. The light wasn't always on in here as the bulbs always blew, so I expected it to be dark. There was a dingy, little wooden chandelier in here and only one of the bulbs worked, it wasn't very powerful, so it was very dark still. The noise suddenly stopped. I didn't want to venture in further, so hastily left the room, closed the door behind me and stood back in the hallway. All of the lights went out, but I didn't seem to mind. The moonlight now brighter than the street lamp, shone eerily into the hallway, refracting light in every possible direction. I approached the front door to check it was locked and thought to myself, how shiny and bright the light was. The door was locked, so I turned around as if to go back upstairs to bed. There was a figure sat on the stairs, looking at me. I could see the moonlight reflect in its eyes. "Oh dad!" I exclaimed, "What are you doing? I thought it was a ghost or..." my attention suddenly drawn back to the moonlight on the door behind me, the effervescence somehow taking over my mind. When I turned back a split second later, there was no one there. The figure had gone. I assumed my father had just gone back up the stairs to bed. I felt a little nervous, so I ran up the stairs taking two steps at a time. I could still do this very quietly, as I was very nimble on my feet. I always wanted to get to my room as quickly as possible. I didn't see the light on under my dad's door, which was sometimes ajar – I peeked in and he was fast asleep, in bed. I thought back to the shiny eyes in the dark and felt a cold realisation, Laura wasn't home for the night, so what was it? Something else was in the house. I freaked out, heart rate increased, and I flung myself into my bed, quilt wrapped tightly around me in every place and completely covering my head and face. I stayed there until I drifted off to sleep.

My dreams were not always awful, there were times when they were incredible. I would fly and soar above trees. I had incredible adventures in my mind. I would dream of music as if it was messages to listen to, certain songs to bring out different emotions in me. I felt the glow of warmth and love – it just made the reality I lived in even more grotesque I suppose. That night wasn't one of those nights.

"Shhhh", hissed a voice, echoing in the darkness. Unexpectedly awake, I clenched my quilt tighter around me. "Listennnn…" a voice lingered, as suddenly the quilt was wrenched from my hands and pulled half off of me. I yelped out in the dark and pulled it back, as an unseen force struggled with me. I grabbed for it in the darkness as it was tugged again. "What do you want from me?!" I yelled into the darkness. I wished the curtains had been opened, so at least there would be streetlight or moonlight. I felt the strength of whatever it was shaking my bed and holding me down, I was suddenly unable to move. There was a pressure on my chest and I couldn't move. It felt like whatever was there, wanted me out. I didn't know how to process what I was feeling, I was a young child still reeling from physical and mental trauma. I had moved to a house that felt as if it had a heavy darkness to it. I can't explain what it was like, but I feared going around it in the dark when I had to feel for the light switches. A constant pressure and spying. Even if I was sat listening to the radio or recording songs, it was like something was just there, watching. Something invisible held me flat against the bed, I screamed until I thought my lungs would burst, but no sound came out now. I was restricted in every way. There was nothing but silence from my mouth, as the voice swirled around my mind. There was laughing now, distant and muffled, but it was certainly there. A light suddenly came on in the hallway, but it began to grow in brightness as I turned my eyes to the side, to see. My eyes were the only things I could move. The light grew brighter until it filled the whole frame around my door. I heard laughter. The volume of giggles increased, sinister and playful at the same time. Like a hazy recollection of childhood play. All of a sudden the laughter turned to screams, they were shrill and ear piercing. I felt my body lift and in that second, I was on my feet, pulling at the door handle. I struggled with it and fell back onto the floor as the door swung open. I looked into the black hallway, nothing but darkness stared ominously back at me. Before I had seen it or had time to think, a decayed arm appeared from under the bed, crawling on its crumbling fingers towards me. Small fragments of skin fell to the floor as small blisters and pustules burst on the surface of the arm. The nails crumbled, as it eased its way out towards me in the darkness. Each nail turning to flakes and dust, as it fragmented and dissipated into the air. The fingers opened, poised and ready to take a hold. It grabbed my leg and pulled me under the bed, before I could even let out a small yelp. I was instantly ripped to pieces under there, clawing to get out but in total silence. Nothing was left, except blood and stains on the underside of the mattress. I awoke, soaked with sweat and breathing heavily again. I laid there, deep in the moment and thinking, not again.

I always felt attracted to the strange back room downstairs. I remember recording my tapes and sometimes wondered if ghostly voices would appear on them. I would later come to learn that this was called EVP, Electronic Voice Phenomenon. I once recorded my own voice and then slowed it down for Halloween, it was so sinister though that I felt like I was calling on something. I remember hearing my own maniacal laughter slowed down and thinking that it was a bit too much. My friends came over to play basketball or ride bikes down to town or to Tehidy. I would cycle or walk to Redruth to visit my best friend Hannah. All those years on and we were still friends. When I was at my mum's, I had gotten into stop motion and I had created my own Wallace and Gromit films, where I stopped the camera, moved a little piece and then carried this on. I was very creative and enjoyed doing things like this. I even went as far as trying to build and replicate the Wallace and Gromit house, so that I could put the characters in there – it took ages, and I drew each individual bone on Gromit's wall. I was very proud of my work. There was also no Alison around, destroying the things I was making. I always had the sense of being watched while I did all of this though. The house vibed at me and I vibed at it back. I felt as if there was something that wanted me out or wanted me, it wanted to frighten me. I sometimes wondered if it was my own imagination, because of the years I had actual fear of the beatings etcetera, maybe now there was none of that happening, I was creating fear as it was what I was used to feeling. What was I without it?

Out in the garden under the brilliant sunshine, I used to play with my Pogs or whatever I had collected at the time. Every now and then, when I was out in the back garden, I would get an urge to look up to the back windows of the house. In my mind's eye, I would imagine that if I looked up that I would see a horrible face or something, so I never looked. I spent a lot of time cycling out on my own, just enjoying the freedom, going through Tehidy woods. Through all the bluebells, depending on the season. I used to go down to the Tolgus Valley on the A30, which had a huge viaduct over it – it must have been 200 feet high. I'd ride under that and push my bike up the big hills, then attempt to ride them down.

Sometimes I would fall off and hurt myself, but that was normal. That was part of growing up, normally. I still didn't have hundreds of friends, as I guess I hadn't socialised as well as other children had. I was quite introverted and just did my own thing, but I was okay with this though. I had a few friends though and we would hang out whenever we could. The woods stretched for miles and miles, filled with ancient oaks and beeches. There was one special tree; the twisted tree, everyone called it, where people carved their names in love hearts or just dated it to show they had been there. Waterways glistened and small lakes and ponds reminded me of a childhood time before I ever met Alison or experienced that, when I had swum there in that small pool with a little Aztec, granite waterfall placed on a mound, before they became over grown and tangled with weeds and nettles. I don't know how old I was then, but I remembered it with a fondness and a wonderful sense of warmth. I would go camping in the tent my mum had brought me. Sometimes in the garden, sometimes at my mum's on the concrete veranda. I remember one night, there was a horrific thunderstorm and lightening. There I was, sleeping in my tent, while they all freaked out inside the house. I used to listen to my Walkman all the time. Tracks I often had on my tape loop were, Jam and Spoon, "Right in the night", TLC, "Waterfalls", Whigfield, "When I think of you", Robert Miles, "Children" and "One and One", Living Joy, "Dreamer", Scatman, Maria Nayler, "Angry Skies". I often played my cassette of N-Trance's B side, "Take you There." For me, it was a mixture of epic dance music with soaring dark beats, and lyrics I could purely relate to, "Oceans of the world surrounding me. I'm drifting like a wave upon the sea. I'll treasure every moment in my life…".

I began to get into a little bit of Drum and Bass. Baby D's "I Need your Loving" was so good to me. I felt a spiritual draw to it in the words, "I need your loving, like the sunshine. Everybody's gotta learn sometime…". I would play it repeatedly, rewinding the tape maybe twenty times and listening to it over and over. I got more and more into dance music at this point. I would spend the time alone in my room, dancing to the music and pretending that I was the person performing the songs. Living a dream, where I was a famous star and could reach people with my music. I could be anything I wanted to be. So many songs at this point influenced me, they taught me about life and experience. Jinny, "Keep warm" and Corona were constantly on the radio. A classmate brought in a cassette with Love City Groove on it and I immediately attached myself to it. It wasn't often that someone else introduced me to new music, but I was very gracious at hearing it. I would imagine I was dancing and playing these songs to thousands of people on massive stages. I was the dance guru in my fantasies, singing songs like Strike's "You Sure Do", The Original, "I Love You, Baby", The Night Train; Jam and Spoon, "Right in the Night", D'Lacey, "Hideaway", Technohead, "I Want to be a Hippy", The Bucketheads, "These Sounds Fall into my Mind", The Real McCoy, "Runaway". I wanted to run away and save my life, just as the lyrics said. I longed to learn to play an instrument of some kind and felt particularly close to slower, more guitar-based songs. I liked rock music as well. I had such a broad taste. The Connells, "'74,'75", Scarlet, "Independent Love Song", Kylie, "Confide in Me" and "Where the Wild Roses Grow", were also songs that shaped me around that time. Just songs that were stories, things I could relate to, pure dreamscape and escapism. As I would arrive home, I would dismount my bike and take off the headphones that covered my ears. For all its beauty, every time I came home and dismounted my bike, the fear crept in again. A dark foreboding which drew my eyes to those windows. The opaque eyes of the house looking for me, waiting for me to come home.

Then 1996 happened. I was obviously into all of my music. It was all chart music, so it covered every genre. I thought that music had hugely triggered me at this point, but I was wrong. I adored the music I listened to, but I wasn't really obsessed. Then in 1996, I was discovering myself, discovering I was gay. This is something that I have no need to discuss further than that, as my private life is for me, but it was a time of revelation for me when I knew who I was and what I wanted. I even remember the first gay kiss on

EastEnders, with my dad turning to me and saying, "If you ever turn out like that, I will chop it off!". Because of that statement, I never told him. I never came out to my father. What a terrible thing for a person to say. Should I have expected anything else? It was just something else in my life I hid from and didn't discuss with him. We were not an open or close family, we already had all of the abuse secrets, so what was one more? It was also about respect, so how could I have faith in someone like that with something so important, when they never respected me? I had zero respect for my father – respect is earned, not given through fear.

I heard the song on the radio, "Wannabe" and I was instantly enchanted. The Spice Girls came at a time when I could have gone either way, I look back and think I was near a mental breakdown. I had taken everything for so long and flown on auto pilot, I didn't see this at the time. Hindsight is a wonderful humbler. I was suddenly rejuvenated and obsessed, I collected all the cut-outs from the newspapers and made little scrap books. I brought the magazines for the posters. Everything I could get my hands on, I did. The music took me away to another place. Especially the B-side to "Say you'll be there", "Take me Home". I watched them on every channel I could, every interview. I longed to see my idols live. I had a dream to meet them as well, but that's a harder one to fulfil. Who would have predicted that nearly twenty-five years later, that dream would come true? I had a very broad range of musical tastes, but I wanted every cassette they released. They were my prized possessions. I was even happy at Christmas as my dad, under Laura's orders, got me their album Spice for Christmas. They were my favourite band. I loved these girls – they just did what they wanted and didn't care. That was the appeal. The energy. I even deconstructed my Wallace and Gromit plasticine creations and made all five of the spice girls. I watched them on the 1997 Brit Awards. Geri Halliwell in her Union Jack dress was an iconic moment. I was so obsessed with these girls, that nothing else mattered. I gathered every item I could find and/or afford.

The biggest moment of my life in that house approached. It wasn't a pleasant experience and for a long time I blocked it, and when it seeped out of my memory, I denied it with abject fear. I always felt like the house at Agar Road was calling me back from wherever I was. Or there was something in there that wanted me. I didn't know. I read a lot and all I could imagine was that it was a horrific ghost and if I saw it, I would literally die. It was total fear of the unknown. Every dream I had that involved the eerie light emanating from under my door, I would feel absolute dread. Sometimes, I would open the door and it would be dark. Other times, I would open the door and the light would move down the hallway, down the stairs and then out of sight. I felt fear, but followed anyway. I would go out through the back of the house into the garden and then my knees would begin to tremble. Something would urge me to turn around and investigate the windows of the house, but I never did. I couldn't. I wouldn't. If I dreamt, I was in the bathroom, then it was always the same thing. I would be in the bath with my back to the glass panels in the door. Something always tugged me under the water, and I would wake up wet and hot.

A few days before my 14th birthday my father yet again confirmed his dodgy dealing lifestyle by saying he was off to France for the night. "Why are you going to France?" I questioned, "Cheap fags and booze", my deceptive father replied as he dug through a drawer looking for his passport. "Arrrrgh, where the fuck is it?" my father screamed, his face turning as red as tomato sauce. All of a sudden, I felt the familiar sickness in the pit of my stomach. I hadn't felt that for a while. I had almost got too comfortable at not being in trouble. How full of myself for getting above my station. I should have known. It hit me like a brick wall. I was instantly back in the moment of horror I used to live through at West Park and Plain-an-Gwarry. My father turned as quick as a blink and punched me right in the side of the head, screaming, "Where is it, you little bastard, where the fuck have you put my passport?" Oh, what a poor boy I was. I just lay sobbing on the floor, unable to breathe, frozen with the fear of being hit again. It wasn't long before Trevor found the passport, although he didn't apologise before he went.

It was early evening when I was left alone in the house. I watched Trevor leave through the blinds of the living room, get in the car and speed off into the lowering dusky sky, disappearing. I had gotten used to this over the years. I had pretty much brought myself up with very little input. My sister was more of a parent to me than he was. It was a shame, as I was a very intelligent, resourceful young man, but chances were few and far between for any sort of decent life for me. Once my father had left, I locked the front door and left the key in it. I always did this, as there was a constant thought in the back of my mind that it would be quicker and easier to escape if something happened. As a boy, I wasn't worried about people breaking in, I was more worried about what could already be there that could stop me getting out. Maybe it was something in my head that told me to be on edge, but I was always wondering in the back of my mind if something would happen. When Trevor or Laura weren't there, I was very capable of cooking for myself. I looked after Sasha the dog and ran the house from day to day, cleaning the house, doing some of the gardening. Feeding the dog and cleaning her bedding and the small area she was usually in outside. My dad neglected her so much, she was often shut out at night in this tiny little porch, wet and dirty. I would sneak her in most of the time when she wasn't trying to eat my pet hamsters. I noticed that the house was very quiet which wasn't abnormal, so I switched on my radio, blasting away the silence and filling the air with a little bit of joy and vitality. I could hear the songs pass as I dawdled around the house. Billy Ray Martin, "Loving Arms" played full blast, followed by Babylon Zoo, "Spaceman". Sheryl Crow and her guitar came on next and I often thought I'd love to be able to play the guitar like she did. "If it makes you happy, it can't be that bad". The words stuck with me as I thought, if the things I did made me happy then what was the problem? As long as I didn't hurt anybody. Unlike my father.

I decided that I would go out and visit Hannah and Sarah for an hour or two, then come back and finish my schoolwork before the due dates the following week. We just hung out in the local field apposite Safeway's singing songs and swinging on the swings. We had a few drinks. One of us had pinched some vodka off of our parents. We all shared this. We Played Babybird, "You're Gorgeous", OMC, "How Bizarre", The Fugees, "Ready or Not", "No Woman, No Cry", Donna Lewis, "I Love You, Always Forever". We danced to the Lisa Marie Experience, "Keep on Jumping" and to the dance song BBE, "Seven Days and One Week." We ended the evening with a little kumbaya version of Joan Osbornes, "One of Us". These were all songs that I stored in my memory banks, the songs that would travel with me through the rest of my life. Songs that I could reflect on and return to at a moment's notice. After going to see my friends for those few precious shots of underage vodka and laughing until tears streaked down our faces, I returned home.

I walked up the road towards the house bathed in the orange glow of the streetlamps that lit my way. Looking up at the house as I approached, I felt it looked sinister, like something wasn't right about it. Something was different. It was as if there were lots of eyes watching me from every window. Staring straight into my soul, unearthing all the secrets of the abuse I had witnessed and endured for those previous years. The tree outside the property cast unearthly shadows in the streetlights and the branches hung in crooked rows, like barbed wire waiting to ensnare a victim. I pushed the key in the door and it gave the old familiar click as it opened. I felt the whoosh of warm air as I entered. In fact, it wasn't just warm, it was hot. This was very odd as I was sure the house was usually quite cold, and I hadn't even had the heating on. I had left the dog inside, so she was running up and down the hallway happily. I stroked the dog firmly and lovingly, my one true friend who would never judge and would be there on the long, cold nights. Entering the lounge, I noticed the gas fire was on and on full. "How very odd!" I thought to myself, "that was off when I had gone out", I muttered to myself. My father wasn't in the country, Laura was out with her friends and the dog certainly hadn't done it. I just assumed that I must have left it on. I did wonder if something else had turned it on to burn the house down. I had been watching The X Files quite a lot, so was creeped out by everything. My imagination always ran wild, though when I got the feelings in that house, I knew they were real. The thoughts of all the dreams and odd occurrences, the nightmares and voices were cast aside for now. I went into my bedroom downstairs, turned the music up as loud as I could without the neighbours complaining and filled the house with a little bit of Spice. My salvation. I played the cassette over and over, at the time I didn't get a lot of the songs, but later on I would. Some of them were very suggestive as songs usually are, you don't think of that when you're young.

I fed the dog, made sure she went out to the toilet as I didn't want any more small, brown presents that I'd trodden in when the dog was a sparkling little puppy with floppy ears and wagging tail. I finished my work and settled down for the night. The music filled my ears, making me forget every issue I had ever encountered. I went up the stairs feeling the patterned wallpaper as I climbed and ran the bath, filling the room with steam and the bath with bubbles. The water flowed from the two silver water fountains until the bath was three quarters full. I undressed and put my foot into the hot water. "Ouch, shit!" I exclaimed, as I pulled my foot out. It was far too hot, as if the immersion had been left on too long. Everything in the house seemed very hot now, like an energy was burning up inside. I looked down at my foot, which had instantly turned a bit red. This wasn't unusual as I normally got into the bath and kept topping it up with hot water, making it as hot as possible until I was nearly boiled like a crab in a pot. I lit my sister's scented candle, turned off the lights in the bathroom and the hallway, then relaxed into the bath. The music in the background was muffled by the door being closed, but I could still hear it as I lay back. I rested my head on the back of the tub and closed my eyes, breathing in the steam and feeling extremely relaxed. I listened to the music coming from down stairs. Klubheads, "Klubhopping", followed by Space, "The Female of the Species". I always thought that song was funny, as Alison was a female and she was a lot more deadly than the male that I knew. She had incited most of my punishments from back along, so in fact she was worse than Trevor. If she hadn't created the opportunity, then he may not have acted so badly towards me.

About five or ten minutes had passed when I twitched myself awake. I thought it had only been a few seconds that I'd drifted off, but I had slipped a little into the tub, which caused me to wake up. Everything was silent in the flickering candlelight. I suddenly realised that I couldn't hear the radio anymore and I knew that the tape lasted well over an hour, so it couldn't have finished yet. The light was off in the hallway and the bathroom, so I couldn't tell if it was the electric that had gone out. I wondered if the electric meter under the stairs had run out and caused the radio to go off. I called out to the dog, who I heard outside the bathroom door, move and then resettle down. Once again, I turned the hot water tap on and topped the water up, melting into the loveliness of the heat. Continuing to soak in the bath, I couldn't get the thought of the radio out of my mind, so I got out of the bath, pulled the cord for the bathroom light and it flickered into life immediately. "Hmmmmm", I thought to myself, the electric obviously hadn't run out, no power cut. I grabbed my towel from the rail and opened the bathroom door. Again, the hallway felt very warm like when I had first come into the house. Wrapping the towel around me as I made my way to the top of the stairs, I heard a sound that was familiar, but I didn't latch onto what it was straight away. I went down the stairs leaving wet footprints behind me as I went, and walked into the lounge. The gas heater was on again. On full blast. A tingle of uncertainty went up my spine. The dog followed along happily, not seeming to notice any change in atmosphere, but all the hair stood up on the back of my neck. Feeling slightly bemused, I went to my bedroom and found that the radio had actually been turned off. The button had been pushed in so it had not done it automatically or as the result of a quick power cut. A strange feeling crept over me, I had the feeling that came over me quite often. It was something that filled me with fear, because I didn't really understand what it was or want to know what it was. Time had passed and I still didn't understand it any more than I had before. All I knew was that some feelings made me feel very uncomfortable and I often felt those eyes were burning into me. It was almost as if someone was stood directly behind me, eyes boring into the back of my skull. When I moved, it moved, so I could never catch sight of it.

"Someone's walked over your grave", I said out loud as I looked down at the dog, wagging her tail expectantly at me. I kept feeling the brush of cold and eyes across my back the whole evening, but ignored it. There was something odd that appeared to be following me around the house, as if it was attached to me. There wasn't a moment when living in that house that I felt like it wasn't empty. Like there was always something somewhere in one part of the house. If I was upstairs, I often felt it peering at me through the crack of the door. When I was in the kitchen, it would be out in the back garden area. If I was in the lounge, it was in the hallway and the room down to the kitchen. I would have to turn all the lights on at night and almost run down that hallway to the kitchen. By now this wasn't an unusual occurrence, strange things had been happening to me for a long time. I sometimes wondered if I had become so paranoid from years of being mentally and physically abused, that maybe I was always waiting for something to happen. Or maybe I was some sort of schizophrenic. Now it wasn't happening in real life, maybe I was somehow dreaming this all up. However, I had feelings in my gut and knew things before they happened. Nothing fantastical or major, but little subtle things. I would later find out these were small synchronicities. The feelings had become so familiar to me, even at that age, just like other things in my life that

I had become used to. I often thought how weird it was that someone should have to get used to these sorts of things. I noticed that a lot of my friends didn't want to stay in 138 Agar Road for very long. Hell, even I didn't want to stay there very long, but I had no choice.

The house sucked the soul and the air from my body. There was a darkness to the property, it just hung in the air. An unhappiness. I was young and naïve and really didn't understand it, but I had a strange fascination with the macabre and ghost stories and such. I hadn't felt this way about any of the other houses I had lived in as a child, so I assumed that good energy could also be absorbed into a home and that's why some places feel warm. Others can feel desolate and cold, that's because they absorb bad energy. I thought to myself suddenly about how nightmarish my dreams had recently become and whilst I was doing well at school, I was socially awkward which was stressful in itself. I wondered if this was the cause of the dreams or the constant stress of living with a terrible parent. While I feared Trevor and what he could do, I also did what I wanted, within reason, as he was never around. I guess that was a bit sad, as he never had an input. He never went to parent evenings or had anything to say. That is sad for him that he couldn't take part in his own children's lives, feel the proudness and fulfilment only a parent can feel. He was truly cold and that was a shame for him. I was not like that. I was full of light and full of warmth, still.

In the meantime, my dreams had become increasingly nightmarish and there were always distorted images of people trying to claw towards me for some sort of attention or recognition. I felt like they were trying to crush me, suffocate me. There was too many of them and I couldn't focus on a single one. I could feel them all. I could sense every one of their emotions, picking up on them like sound waves traveling through the air. It was so many mixed feelings and emotions. I thought they seemed to be pleading for help, but the faces, in my minds eye, were so malformed and contorted that it put the fear of God in me. Plus, I could never escape. Sometimes I felt as if I was pinned to the bed, unable to do anything. For someone so young to be experiencing things like this, was very perturbing. I was often running somewhere and then out of the darkness, these spectres with dismembered faces and rotting corpses, would reach out and try to halt my progression to wherever it was I was going. I would wake up soaking with sweat, heart thumping and full of fear. This was something that I never got used to, even though it happened so often. I would always push these thoughts to the back of my mind and focus on something different. I wanted to believe in something paranormal, but from all the programs I had seen on the television, I was afraid. Everything appeared to be negative, so I wasn't sure if it was easier to think I was a crazy schizophrenic or embrace it for what it was.

I was being led to believe that there was some sort of life after death. I didn't really know anything much about death, I hadn't really experienced it. It was more something at this age that had happened to my grandparents and my mum and dad. I just remember people not being around anymore. I don't recall if I was ever told about people passing away. If I was honest,

I don't think my father had ever explained anything to me. I began to feel that this wasn't the only plain of existence, there was something more out there, whether it was pure with light or dark with evilness. There was something. I couldn't say what, but after all my experiences there had to be something, otherwise there was something wrong with me. I had always tried to be cheerful and optimistic. I mean, having a brutal father growing up meant that any time there wasn't a beating, it was pure heaven. Just moments when I was buying my cassettes, recording the Top 40, riding my bike around in the sunshine, the rays of light splitting through the leaves in Tehidy Woods. Just perfect moments of freedom and carefreeness. Even though I had experienced little other than horror or fear, I still looked for the good in people. I wasn't the same as my father. I had the heart of my great-grandmother, my nan and my mum. The funny thing about people is that they do not want to know about something if it doesn't have a positive to it. People tend to shut out what isn't good or what doesn't feel right to them, it must be part of what it is to be human. That's what I did. I was curious about other realms, spirits and ghosts, but at that age I knew nothing other than what I had seen on the television or read in books. I didn't have any real peoples, real accounts of their own experiences and what all of that means.

Everything I felt was like the fear I felt as young child when I would come home, the fear of what my father was going to do to me. The fear was a deeper, darker fear though. The kind of fear where you are afraid to open your eyes in the dark, in case you see something.

In my imagination, I always saw a person looking away from me out of a window and as they would turn to look at me, there would be no face, just a skull and rotting flesh hanging off. I didn't want to see that for real, and I guess my brain overexaggerated these fears. It was a knotting and queasy feeling in the pit of the stomach that took a long time to go away. These feelings came very often, and I began to realise that there was a good reason for them, I was just waiting for some sort of horrific evidence. Some confirmation.

It was starting to get late at this point, and I was alone in the house. It was usual that I would be alone, it was almost a pattern that had followed me throughout my life, and I was comfortable with this feeling. I guess, I never really needed anyone. It was ten past midnight, but I didn't feel tired. I looked at the clock intermittently as if waiting for something or someone to arrive. The dog was fast asleep, so I sat watching her intently for about twenty minutes as she twitched and her little legs jolted out, as if she was chasing rabbits or something. Every now and then, Sasha would let out a small whimper as if she had caught her prey and mouth twitching as if she was eating. I smiled contently to myself. The television was on in the background and was playing a repeat of the Outer Limits, which really used to freak me out with its creepy intro. At this point, the house was completely silent, the tree outside blew gently across the streetlamp so there was a little light coming in from outside. I was so engrossed watching the dog sleep, that I hadn't noticed the faint odour that had begun to fill the room. I soon drifted off to sleep in the corner of the room, by the dog bed.

Opening my eyes sometime later, I looked at where the dog had been and saw that she was gone. She had moved to the door, which was now shut, and was making small whining noises and shivering as if she was cold and scared. She was fast asleep, but the growls and body shakes made me think she was not happy – probably having nightmares about her terrible owner. It was as if an adult dog had been breathing helium and was making little high-pitched growls and barks. I looked up at the lights on the ceiling that had somehow been turned on, and noticed that one of the bulbs had blown again. I'd only replaced them the day before. I didn't remember if I had turned the lights on earlier. I had fallen asleep, so was a little disorientated. Due to the bulb being blown, the others were casting some eerie shadows around the room, but I paid little attention to this. Suddenly my eye was drawn to the corner of the room, it was like one of the shadows had turned into a giant finger. I had that tingle down my spine again. I thought to myself that it was something that wanted me. I could feel it reaching towards me and trying to get inside me. I didn't want that. I felt like it wanted me there. I didn't know for what, but I definitely didn't like it.

I didn't like how the room seemed at night and how the shadows clawed their way towards me. There was something very off about this room. Something very off indeed. I had felt it since I moved into the house. If I could, I would have run past the doorway every time I had to go past. I would have had it nailed shut. It was that intense a feeling. It was always an expectation that something was about to happen. Sometimes I felt my way through the house in the dark if the lights didn't work, afraid that if I opened my eyes, something would get me. Wondering and waiting for the next freaky occurrence to happen. There was always a feeling of expectation in the air as if a charge was building, like before a thunderstorm that would suddenly explode in bright flashes of light and reality. I thought it was very odd that at the age, I would be afraid of the dark. I had dealt with unimaginable trials in the past that no child should ever bear witness to, and I knew deep down I was strong, but the threat of the unknown was always unnerving. As a young man, I could jump off the local cliffs at Portreath into the sea, jump and climb over huge walls, build fires, break into factories and everything. I had dealt with the mental and physical abuse of Trevor and Alison and survived through it, so why should this be any different? I can't explain how different it felt. I was constantly haunted by the thoughts of ghosts and the dead trying to suffocate me in my sleep and weigh me down. I was sure that the intention was not pure and no good would come of contact with any of them. I wasn't educated enough in the realm of the paranormal, so I feared everything. I didn't think logically about it. It was a sort of blind panic. I was so scared, that I never really questioned if I would ever understand it or if it would become less frightening. The sad point was that I had got so used to other sorts of fear and pain, that I just got on with it. Just trundled on doing my thing. Keeping going. My brain was always busy as I tried to get off to sleep. Hiding under the quilt as if that would save me from any attacks. I had a technique that I used to get myself off to sleep, so that I wasn't plagued by all of these thoughts all the time;

breathing in and out, focusing only on this, I cleared my mind of all thoughts – as soon as my eyelids felt heavy, I was gone. Music also helped. I sailed into a blissful, relaxing sleep. That night I settled to sleep as my radio played Ultra Nate, "Free", and then Puff Daddy and Faith Evans, "I'll be Missing You". The clock wrapped around the bed head on bendy legs read 2.53 a.m. and a green light flickered over it, as if some sort of power surge had run through it. It was battery operated. It was a frog and its legs were made of a pipe cleaner type of material, that let it wrap around and cling to most handles or surfaces.

I jolted awake as if something had shaken me. I lay there silently in the darkness with my eyes shut. Everything was silent. There was no sound at all. I remained motionless. I heard a scratching coming from behind my head, but under the bed. I could hear Sasha whimpering and moaning as she bunched herself into the corner under the bed. I felt the hairs go up on the whole of my body. I clenched my eyes shut tighter and wondered why she would have gone under the bed like that. She continued to make these noises, I didn't want to open my eyes or move the quilt. I didn't want to look, I didn't want to know what was there. I felt as if something was in the room. I was scared. The dog was scared. My mind instantly reverted to the thought that it was an attack from Alison, but it was more sinister. She would come in and just smack me and attack me. This was more stealthy. Something just watching from somewhere in the room, I imagined that if I opened my eyes or pulled the quilt down, there would be some sort of monster waiting right in front of me and would pounce. Ah, what a wonderful imagination I had. I put my arm out from under the quilt and felt for my lamp, which was placed right next to the bed. I felt it click under the pressure of my fingers and through the quilt, I could see a faint glow as I dared to open my eyes. The dog was still making faint noises, but wasn't scratching into the corner as much. The cold electric feeling I sometimes got was still there. I thought the light would provide me with some protection and some sort of confidence to jump out of my bed and look around the room. It was only a few seconds that had passed, so I thought it was time to be brave and stop being an idiot. I slowly began to lift the quilt on the wall side, so I was looking at the wall as I removed the quilt. As I did this, I saw a deep, dark shadow cast against the wall. With the light of the lamp, the person had to be stood right over the top of my bed. I felt a surge of urgency as if someone was playing a trick on me and I flicked the whole quilt off me in one go. A sudden realisation dawned on me when I saw that there was no-one in the room, the shadow had gone. The curtains were closed and the door was shut, there was no one in the bedroom. The dog's squeals and moans continued. I could almost feel her shaking against the wooden frame of the bed. I froze for a second, unable to process the black shadow I had just seen. I was beyond petrified. It was crushing. Blinding. Insanity causing panic. I couldn't deny this to myself now. The dog moaning and hiding under the bed was totally out of character. The shadow I had just seen and that had now gone through a closed door. No. I couldn't deny it, however much I tried. My only memory of the next few minutes was me throwing myself back under my quilt, curling into the foetal position with my fingers in my ears and my eyes crunched shut so tightly, not even a vice could have prised them apart. I rocked back and forth, saying internally to myself, "There's nothing there. There's nothing there. There is nothing there!". I remember singing Chumbawumba, "Tubthumping" to myself over and over again. "I get knocked down, but I'll get up again. You're never gonna keep me down". I didn't remember falling asleep, but when I woke up, the room felt normal again. The dog was laid on the end of the bed and I sighed a deep breath of relief. I looked at the clock, it said 5 a.m., so a few hours had passed. I went back to sleep for a short while.

Morning came gratefully to me as I awoke, wrapped in the comfort of my duvet. I recoiled at the thoughts of what had happened the previous night. There was no way I could disbelieve it anymore. There was something else out there. Well, inside where I was, and it felt like the monsters that wanted me were as real as ever. I had seen a shadow of some sorts. I didn't know what it was at that age, but in time to come, I would piece it together that it was a shadow figure I had seen. No-one knows what they are, whether they were human or are demonic. All I knew was that I had seen it as clear as day, and I felt that it was very melancholic and dark. However, this was blacker and infinitely more sinister than anything I had ever experienced. I just felt it inside. I was more than addicted to horror shows or paranormal programs and wondered if this had attracted something in. I read horror books and was just transfixed by anything horrific. No, that wasn't right, as it had been happening since before I could even read. Before I was even aware. I was fascinated, but at the same time, terrified of conjuring up something just by thinking about it. I often thought how silly the things I thought to myself were, as I just seemed to pluck these random ideas out of thin air. Sometimes I knew things, as if I had just been presented with some sort of knowledge. Sometimes I felt things. There was no rhyme nor reason to it, it just happened. It's hard to explain, but when I knew something, it just came out rather than me giving it any actual thought. Almost like verbal diarrhoea.

The shadow figure loomed in my mind. Inside, I felt sick to the core, rocked and frightened by what I had seen. It felt unearthly and I felt like it wanted me. For something awful? I just didn't know. All I was sure of, was that it had happened, I had seen it and I couldn't pretend that I didn't believe anymore. I felt like it was attaching itself to me and the more time I stayed in the house, the more it would grip onto me. I didn't have dark thoughts, but I had a constant fear and a sense of foreboding. I did often feel sad as well, but just assumed this was due to the emotions I was experiencing living in that house and growing taller in more ways. For a long time after this event, I often dreamt about the black figure on my wall. It would stretch out and reach towards me. I would feel my insides boiling with the pressure and would wake up gasping just before the dim, shadowy fingers touched my skin. From time to time in my mind, I would see the shadow moving away from the wall, down the hallway and out to the garden, as if trying to draw me out there alone. I was wise to its deceptions and misleading. It wanted me to follow. That's what demons do, lead you astray and then steal your light and soul. Then when I was outside, it was like it was going inside trying to lead me in, drawing my eye. There must have been a reason for this. It was almost like something repeating over and over through the years, as if waiting for someone to notice. I wasn't even sure if I would imagine all of this or if it was meant for me to see. If I wasn't there, would this shadow re-enact its route and keep moving anyway? Was it waiting for someone to follow and discover what was going on? Or someone to lead away, into obscurity, never to be seen again? It never felt good to me. I never relaxed in that house. I was always on my guard. It was part of who I was at that point, always alert and waiting for trouble.

I decided to take Sasha down to Tehidy woods. As I got onto my bike, I put on my old faithful Walkman. The headphones were getting a bit worn, but it all still worked fine - I got lost in the music as I rode. I listened to No Doubt, "Don't Speak", Gala, "Freed from Desire", Tori Amos, "Professional Widow", Tina Moore, "Never Gonna Let You Go" and Rosie Gaines, "Closer than Close". I listened to every song eagerly when I wasn't listening to the Spice Girls. It was quite a long ride, as I had gone the long way whilst lost in the music. The breeze blowing on my face and through my hair as I headed down through the valley. Up the other side by the three mine stacks and down through Illogan to get to the far end of Tehidy. I had plenty of free time, so I rode for hours. I just played songs and sung to myself as I went. I played Hanson, "Where's the Love?", Danni Minogue, "All I Wanna Do", Blueboy, "Remember me" and Sash featuring La Trec, "Stay". I particularly loved that song as it was about finding someone and wanting them to stay – I was feeling like that's all I needed in my future life. Something or someone to complete me. If I only knew then that I didn't need anyone except myself to complete me. "I had a dream last night, you were there. You held my hand so tight. I thought I'd just die!" I used to sing as loudly as I could.

Sometimes people would look on at me smiling or looking, frowning disapprovingly as I flew past on my bike, bellowing songs. It was what was needed. Tehidy was always a magical place for me. When I was smaller, it seemed endless. I loved how the sun shone through the green leaves in the summer. I would bask in the light and purity of it all. I had gone there many times since I was a small child and had the vaguest memories of playing in the babbling rivers, waterfalls and in the circular pond that used to be overrun with frogs. The sounds of the ducks and the swans, that were always present in the area. Squirrels galore and clean, flowing water. I always felt connected with nature and grounded when I could embrace it. The trees were old and wise and reached towards the light. The water was loud and persistent, always rolling on. Sasha the dog was an obedient little soul, she doted on the love and attention she got from me when she was allowed in the house or when we were out walking. She would always run alongside the bike as I rode. She was another thing that Trevor could control. She was often shut outside in the wet, cold and mud. I wondered if she was as lonely as I had often felt. We always had a lovely connection and she muffled my tears as well as come to me when I needed to get out for a walk or a run and vent. She was a dear, faithful friend. We were bonded through our mutual survival. That was us. Survivors. Trevor just didn't care about her or look after her, let alone walk her or anything. I had an affinity with animals and was always drawn to them. I loved nature and everything it contained.

I always admired the sun light as it shone through the green canopy of the woods and green leaves. The rays parting and casting shadows throughout the area below. There was something special about the place I grew up, its thick woodlands, coastal paths and plunging valleys. It had mystical rock formations and bronze age settlements, mining heritage and soaring coastal moors. It was and is just beautiful. Stunning in the heat of the summer sun and glorious as storms roll in during the winter. Calm green seas to thrashing, crashing swells. I always felt content and recharged, just by sitting in nature. Absorbing the energy before returning home.

I don't recall us living at Agar Road for very long after the shadow event, as I called it. I wasn't sure if I had mentally blocked how I felt in that house after the incident or if we just moved quickly. We always seemed to be moving very quickly. Usually I'd go to school and by the time the day had ended, I was being taken to a new place. Nothing was constant. I had never told Laura or Trevor about what I'd seen, but I was sure they too had picked up on things happening in that house. Maybe they had had the same visitor. It was another of those days and we were being moved again. Even further away from my friends than before, to Glyngarth at the bottom of Pennance Lane in Lanner. By 1997, I had moved into my fifth home. Thankfully, I left the shadow person behind. As I had moved again, I lost touch with a lot of friends outside of school so was isolated again. I did have my bike and some very close friends, so it wasn't too bad. We all mostly hung out in school and I spent a lot of time alone in Lanner. I was so used to this, but I was always occupied anyway, it was another area for me to explore. I found different routes up to the local quarries on both sides of Lanner and would either walk up there or ride my bike. I would revisit Bell Lane, where my great grandparents had lived. My mum once told me a story about how harsh my great grandfather could be and had caused my great gran to put her head in the oven one day, in an attempted suicide. She doted on us grandchildren. I remember poking the head of his walking stick around the door one day and he flew up out of the chair and sent me flying across the room. He was not happy about it. We were never meant to touch things while we were there. They had both passed away so there was nowhere to actually visit, but as I passed by on my bike, I would pay a silent homage. The new house did not feel at all like Agar Road. It felt warmer. It felt empty, as if there wasn't anything stored within its walls. There was no sense of anxiety or underlying fear. I wasn't afraid and there was no feeling of impending doom. I was growing a little older and doing my own thing. Time began to change as I grew. My sister grew. The whole family grew. Trevor remained in his rut, taking advantage of people, only helping those with whom he had a use for. My musical tastes also developed. I began to love more rockier music and was falling in love with all sorts of upbeat remixes of all types of songs. I used to play and sing to Meredith Brooks, "Bitch" everywhere I went for a while, letting the tape flick back and forth. Technology was also changing and I decided I needed a CD Walkman. I am ashamed to say that I couldn't afford one of these, so I stole it. I take full responsibility for this, but I partially blame my father for instilling such awful behaviour in me from a very young age. My karma came when it needed eight batteries and the Walkman only needed two, so I often stuck with the Walkman. When I rode my bike, the CD's would also skip. Then one day it flew out of my pocket and smashed in the road. That was my comeuppance.

Chapter 5

Realisation and running blind

Turning of the mind,
Turning of a page,
What happens when the sun sets?
When all you have inside is rage

<u>Glyngarth, Lanner 1997</u>

Dance music played throughout the house; Dario G, "Sunchyme", DJ Quicksilver, "Bellissima", Olive, "You're Not Alone", All Saints, "Never Ever" club mix. I had collected the ring pulls off of the Pepsi cans for a free Spice Girls CD, "Step to me". By the age of 14, my life had changed considerably. I was still obsessed with the Spice Girls. I had become a bit of a kleptomaniac and would steal money out of my dad's friend's big whiskey bottle. He was staying with us for some reason, but was a bit of a pervert. I found loads of porno mags in the bedroom he had downstairs. My sister was sure he had spied on her in the shower as well, by looking through the key hole in the door. I took all the money to spend on Spice Girls posters, photos, books, CD's, anything I could get my hands on. It was at this time in my life that I became more aware of the pressure my dad would put on my sister. I was sure he would constantly gamble the rent money away and it wasn't very often he did a big shop to feed us all. I remember mainly being given chips and beans and I would have to cook myself pasta cheese and beans more often than not. I used to go across the road to the bakery as well to feed myself. Trevor would try to coerce Laura into having the rent and bills all in her name. That was the ultimate control. He would end up paying nothing and she would be blacklisted. He was probably trying to do this as he had already been blacklisted. He was not a reliable person. Laura didn't stay around much longer after that. I heard them having a blazing row one night and a cup smashing. I later learnt he had lost his temper and thrown it at her. There was a glimmer of the real Trevor I hadn't seen for a while. I remember walking into her bedroom and catching her packing her stuff up in preparation to move out. There was no way she would stay with him around. I envied her for being able and strong enough to get away. I didn't know when she was going, but I knew it was inevitable. I knew she would leave me there, but I could totally understand. My father was still seeing Alison, but I often went out if I knew she was coming or she would visit him when I was at my mum's house. I spent my time hanging out with Hannah and other friends.

It was a strange old life, I just lived day to day, trying to hang out with friends and muddle through. We all had various little parties or got drunk down at the park. When I was on my own, I was quite happy being self-motivated and doing my own thing. I would often go out further and further exploring on my bike. I would meet up with friends in Redruth, then later cycle back. It was excellent exercise. I used to cycle up the huge hill at the back of my house instead of the hill on the main road. It was steeper, but then the top part that joined on was flatter. I would cycle down Lanner Hill at thirty miles an hour sometimes. I was fearless then when it came to the freedom of being on two wheels. Sometimes I would bypass this route completely and go over the top of Carn Marth quarry that eventually joined onto the back lanes towards St Day village and looped back to Redruth. Like Carn Brea, Carn Marth was high on a hill and you could see all around for miles. You could see in all directions, from Stithians lake and reservoir, to St Austell. There was a couple of old quarries there. One was now full of water and people went up there fishing and camping. The other had sheer walls and was used as an amphitheatre, small plays would be held there. My friends and I used to have a competition, we would play a song like Mousse T, "Horny" or Aqua "Dr. Jones". I had the Antiloop remix that I remember asking my mum to play on some trips from her house to home. As it was getting dark, I'd listen to the dance beats and imagine I was at a club as all the street lamps and car head lights whizzed by. The songs were basically timers. We would see if we could climb up and back down the quarry before the song ended. This was a test that nearly ended in disaster, but no-one was ever hurt. It was a very tranquil and peaceful place that I enjoyed visiting quite often. It was here that Hannah and a few other school friends came. Another boy I knew called Matthew Bonnar threw a rock at the lake, which hit me in the face. I never knew if it was purposeful, but if it was, he was long forgiven. If it wasn't, then all was well either way. Matthew and I had known each other for a long time anyway, we had gone through primary and junior school together. I knew there was no malice and later in life we would be good friends. Hannah and I would hang around the lane at school on breaks smoking and laughing with our friends.

I threw myself into my schoolwork and sailed through my classes, even though my teachers knew I was troubled. At that moment in time, I didn't really feel that troubled. I guess I was just surviving. My brain had not matured enough to process every feeling and emotion that I had within me. I didn't know any better, so just carried on. I must have had some sort of childhood depression or PTSD as I would often skive off school and just go to sleep in my tent in the garden at home. They took pity on me, but enjoyed teaching me because I still did what I should, even though I was barely there. Laura caught me skiving in my tent one day in the garden and marched me to school, holding my hand the whole way into the classroom. I was not impressed by this and went a lot more often. I spent 90% of my time alone in Lanner, listening to music or doing my own cleaning, tidying, hobbies and playing with the dog. I would ride my bike to Redruth or some friends would come down to see me. Sometimes when putting our bikes in the garage, I would run out too quickly, forgetting they were behind me and pull the garage door down. I knocked my friend unconscious once. We laughed about it afterwards. We used to joke about and wonder "What's she gonna look like with a chimney on her?". We didn't even know what the song meant – I still don't. We just wondered why she had a chimney on her. Maybe she was the wicked witch and she had the house land on her, like in The Wizard of Oz. I listened to a lot of Catatonia. I felt that "Road Rage" reflected who I was at that moment. I should have been taking it easy on myself. It wasn't over. Full of rage and potentially losing my mind.

As I settled into that house, I noticed that it did not feel strange. There was nothing off or odd about it, it actually felt like a home. I felt happy there. I had all my toys. My Mighty Maxes. My Lego. My Spice Girls. Laura was just about departed which did not improve Trevor's mood, but he must have known deep down the real reason she had gone. He knew she left because of him. He would never have admitted that to anyone else, but he knew. She did not look back. After that moment, she barely spoke to him ever again. He was not welcome at her wedding and he certainly did not know in years to come that he had grandchildren. The brutality had left its imprint on Laura and she did not wish to revisit any of those terrible, painful memories. So, with my music, my school work and some friends, I ploughed on forward. As I began to understand more about relationships and love, I did feel alone as I didn't know how to come out, whom I could tell or how they would respond. It was still a very taboo subject for someone of my age back then. Plus, I thought people would bully me and beat the crap out of me. I had inherited my dad's temper, so knew if anyone came after me then I would give as good as I got. I didn't have girlfriends like the rest. I was socially awkward, so it was lonely at times. In the deepest moments of despair as I internally healed from my mental wounds, the loneliness crippled me so much that I cried myself to sleep, wondering why I didn't have anyone and why no-one loved me. I was an emotional teenager, full of hormones and rage. The next day whenever I woke up, I would pull up my socks and carry on. I cleaned the house, I walked the dog. I even cleaned out the pond at the top of the garden. I got a bit obsessive over this, but my father never really noticed as he was never there. I ended up setting fire to the garden as I found a drum of his petrol that I decided to shake around the place. I guess on some level, I was out of control. On another, I was just doing what I wanted as I had no parental input. By this age it was like I had two separate lives. The me I had to be when I was at home with Trevor, and the me who I was when I was at my mother's. They never spoke to me and Laura about any of the abuse. They never asked if I was alright or anything. It was kind of like an undiscussed secret. I clearly had been deeply affected and acted out in ways that were violent, aggressive and huge calls for help. I learnt to look after number one.

I still had these random instances when I would feel the hair on the back of my neck go up. I would have extremely vivid dreams that felt real, as if I had just watched a film or something. So many odd experiences that I shrugged off, as they felt very distant to me then. As if I was watching them happening to someone else. The memory of the shadow person faded, as I hadn't experienced anything sinister for a very long while. I continued to read a lot of books about the paranormal, stone tape theory, parallel dimensions and ghosts. So many stories spread over so many years. I had gone from not believing, to fully believing and then to be back in total denial. I always had an image in mind that if I was to accept myself and open myself up, then I would see something that would terrify me. I was convinced. More than the shadow man or Alison's gleaming face in the darkness. I couldn't see what it was, but in my mind, it was disturbing. It would scare me to death.

One evening I was doing chores around the house when a news bulletin came on the TV. "Breaking news, a body has been found in Tehidy woods near Redruth in Cornwall. The body appears to have been there for quite some time, there are no more details at this stage, but it is not a modern site. A local man and his three dogs came across it in the woods of Tehidy, the owner only realised what it was when one of his dogs ran up to him with a human femur bone in its mouth.". The newsreader continued, "The cause of death is yet unknown, but it would appear from initial police reports that the man may have been murdered or committed suicide, due to a suspected cause of death via shotgun. It is unclear. The clothing of the man and items found on and around the body suggest that the body may have been there for over a hundred years. We will bring you more updates when we receive more information.". Something engaged me with this story. Maybe it was because it was so local. It was just up the road, a few miles away. The story was headline news for the next couple of weeks. To be honest, there wasn't much else going on in Cornwall at this time. It was usually about sewage on the beach or tourists that were angry with seagulls swooping at their heads. Everyone would have an opinion on who it may have been and what happened. The truth would be that no one knew. It was a lifetime ago and he had laid undiscovered for so long. The gunshot wound was suspicious, and made it look like suicide. Maybe someone had moved the body to hide it and claim an estate or cover up a wrongdoing. No one could do more than envisage their own scenario. I felt there was something more sinister about it. Something made me ponder how deep his story was. I thought back to some of the dreams I had at that time.

I had had a lot of dreams about running through the woods around that time. I had flashes of a smiling man in the darkness. An arm outstretched as if beckoning me in. It was always the same dream. I was deep in Tehidy woods. It was totally dark as there were no houses nearby. There was moonlight shining above, but very little light managed to creep in down through the canopy. I would be running, faster and faster. I didn't know the route, but I just kept fleeing. Something was coming upon me fast. I never wanted to look back. I moved with such speed that it seemed unreal, as if I was becoming a blur in the dimly lit woods. Dark branches and twigs licked at me as I flew past. Tripping over a root, I would fall into the soft soil, hands sinking into it, face and nose touching it. I felt the damp texture of it against my face, soggy as I inhaled an earthy scent. I didn't have or feel any emotion. Just got straight back up. I would pick myself back up to my feet and continue running. No destination in mind, just journeying further and further from whatever it was that was lurking behind each tree, behind me. Following, watching and stalking. I would always end up in a huge clearing in the middle of Tehidy woods where there were no trees just low grass and moonlight. Then a pain in my brain would explode and I'd wake up. I felt like it was something to do with the man's body that had been found in the woods. I shrugged it off as me being crazy and having had some sort of mental breakdown from the childhood trauma. I sometimes wondered why I had these thoughts and made up such stories. Surely that was all I was doing, making things up in my mind? Giving myself reasons to keep existing and feeling some sort of purpose.

I thought about how my difficult childhood could have left me dead or even more damaged than I already was. In some unimaginable way, that I could be even worse than I was. I severely lacked confidence in regards to people and chatting, making small talk and being socially acceptable. I only really knew how to interact in a bullying sort of aggressive way. I always knew the behaviour wasn't normal and adjusted it accordingly. How could I act any other way with such a poor role model? They say you cannot blame your parents. I blamed mine entirely. I was struggling to change myself because of how they made and moulded me as a child. I knew I'd get back to myself one day. One day.

I did thank my lucky stars that I was still alive, as the beatings from Trevor and Alison could have easily gone too far. I shouldn't say too far, as any beating is a step too far. By too far, I mean they could have killed me. There were multiple times she or he could have easily suffocated me or beaten me to death. I don't actually know how I survived some days. I did often think and hope that one day someone would come and rescue me.

They would stand up for me and settle the score with my father. I hoped that karma would one day visit upon him and Alison, but I had such a negative thought pattern that I didn't really believe it. I never thought karma was real. I wasn't sure how it worked and when it would strike. I just listened when people said that they would get their just desserts. I longed for the day when the balance to my life would be restored and everything would be right. I had survived that far, and I would carry on.

I was a survivor. The path I had been down was not the one I would have chosen, but it was my path and it was mine alone. It was the only one I knew, so I continued. Sometimes I felt that I would be able to handle whatever would be thrown at me down the years. Other times, I felt so alone that I didn't even see a future. I couldn't even imagine ten years' time when things were at their most difficult. I continued on in school. I tried my best and did the work, but was often distracted and disruptive, but I did it in a cheeky way and the teachers still liked me. I did respect them, but I was also free at school to do as I wanted and not be afraid. Whilst I was sat in maths lessons, I would always have my music and headphones on. I used to play all the Bewitched remixes of "Rollercoaster", "To You, I Belong" and "Blame it on the Weatherman". On breaks, we would all gang together and play songs down by the music block. Some of our favourites as a group were, "Ghetto Superstar", Brandy and Monica, "The Boy is Mine", Stardust, "The Music Sounds Better With You" and the latest Madonna album, which was full of amazing songs such as "Frozen", "Ray of Light", "The Power of Goodbye" and "Drowned World/Substitute for Love". That was an album that touched me on a deep level. I listened to it intently every day, dreaming myself away.

In the evenings I would listen to Tin Tin Out, "Here's Where the Story Ends". There was an amazing remix I played continuously. When I was feeling reflective and mourning for the love I didn't have, I would listen to other songs like Billie Myers, "Kiss the Rain", Natalie Imbruglia, "Torn", "Big Mistake", "Pigeons and the Crumbs" and "City". I would listen to Karen Ramirez, "Looking for Love", because that was what I was looking for, longing for. I can honestly say at that age I did not understand what a lot of the songs meant that I was listening to. I was innocent in certain ways. It was only as I grew older and gained experience that I saw the deeper meanings of a lot of these songs. As a child, I had been entranced by the music. As I got older, the music and the lyrics drew me in further. While I slept at night I was only occasionally awoken by vivid dreams. Sometimes I felt that I was being visited by various presences. I was never sure if I was awake or asleep. I was usually somewhere between. I cannot describe how I knew they were different ones, but it was almost as if I felt the energy and each visitor had a different feel, like a fingerprint. I didn't know that years ago, in another time, another house. I never opened my eyes. I would lay there in my bed, frozen in the dark. Passive to the experience. Not breathing. Not making a sound. I would often feel eyes on me. Sometimes they were on the other side of the room. Sometimes it felt as if something was breathing just above me. I always wondered if I opened my eyes, would I see something horrible and distorted ready to unleash fresh terror on me? I would lie frozen in my bed until the sensation left and I felt alone again. I never really questioned any of this as I had grown up with it. The strange feelings were like familiar friends. They came to stay for a while and would disappear again as quickly as they came. I had always believed that in life you dealt with the hand you were given. I wasn't given the best hand, but it was mine. I knew no different. If you are strong enough, you survive. If you aren't, then you will fall at the wayside. I always hoped someone would come and find me, rescue me. I imagined I was a beacon in the dark waiting for that connection, that magnetic attraction. Even at such a young age, I knew what I wanted and what I felt I needed. I always had hope. I was always so full of light and aspiration. Even in the darkest times. The abject fear I would feel. The burning agonies of the beatings. Somehow deep down I did know that everything would change one day. It had to. As that scared boy, I imagined the presence from Agar Road, following me, spreading through the whole of the new house, moving silently and menacingly through the dark in search of something. Comfort? Rest from death? I didn't know, but it didn't feel good. It felt as if it was inside me, rummaging around on a quest for something.

"Here I am..." something faintly whispered in the air. "What?" I remember thinking to myself as I slept. I always recalled thinking to myself that I should wake up. I just couldn't. "Come to me..." a different, more malevolent voice hissed nearby. Barely audible, but there nonetheless. "Come.... to.... me....". The voice repeated the same command over and over again, growing in anger as it hissed into my head and I tried to shut it out with the pillows and quilt. I would still wake up in that state of panic and fear. The dreams were so realistic. I was always back at that house. Always in that room. Had I missed something? Was something trying to reach out and give me a message? I would dream of a dark shape moving from room to room. I felt as if it was looking for me, but I was just a captive audience in my dream. I tried to follow on occasion, but was always woken with a jolt. The dream of that house began to repeat itself. I would be in the hallway with Sasha at my side. Then suddenly it was dark, and I was running. Fleeing, jumping, flying.

Anxiety woke me up. I got up, stretched my legs and decided I'd go out. Trevor had brought a new dog. I was so happy. Finally, Sasha had a friend who would be with her all the time. Even if she didn't like it, it was company for her. He only wanted to play and she was a grumpy old cow. His name was Sabre and he was a beautiful ball of fluff, a long-haired German Shepherd. He was the cutest thing I had ever seen. He was also very naughty, but puppies are. As he was so small, I just took Sasha up to Carn Marth. We dawdled up the hill in a slow fashion. We were crossing the fields a different way to usual. We were going through under growth and tangled nettles. Suddenly the dog came upon a dead horse. It had clearly been there a long time as it was so rotten. I could almost taste how badly it smelt. The skin had peeled back in the sun. It was grotesque. I thought this was very strange as I was used to seeing horses and their riders around where I lived. Would a horse have just died there, what seemed a fair while ago and nobody had noticed? There it lay rotting, decaying and giving off a pungent smell. There was flies and maggots all over what was left of it. The remnants pulsated as eggs hatched underneath the carcass. There wasn't much left of the horse. The skin had obviously rotted away or dried and peeled back. I could see that what remained of the innards had solidified and turned black. With a quick look, I ascertained that the inside was writhing with the sheer number of maggots within. There were flies, buzzing in and out of the carcass, resting on the rib bones as they ate the rotting meat and then whirred inside to lay more eggs. The dog was pulling in anticipation. I tugged Sasha away as I also turned away from this; clasping my hand over my mouth as the smell was far too strong. The dog continued to pull, but I knew if I let go of the dog lead then she would be straight in there. She would stick her face right into the tainted tapestry of death, and then try to lick me – no, thank you! I held my breath, so I didn't have to take in anymore of the blinding fumes.

Something suddenly clicked into place. It was like a chemical reaction in the brain, something linked. Pieces came together. It was like a 'Eureka' lightbulb suddenly flashing on. The dreams I had been having, the putrid smells. Sometimes in my dreams the stench was so foul that I would curl into a ball holding my stomach for fear of vomiting. I had often wondered what that stench was, but had never thought it would be anything real. I often went straight to the thoughts that I was insane and must keep it a secret. I feared if I told anyone they would think I was mad. The horse's pictures that I had found in the shed when we moved into the property at Agar Road were a clue. It was like a weird shrine or a memorial to someone's prized animals. Realisation dawned. What on earth was I thinking about? This story had been placed in my mind, like a knowledge that I had been given. Enlighted to. The thoughts were flooding my mind, drowning my consciousness. It was impossible to think straight there was so many fragments of information whizzing around my head. I didn't even know what I was saying or thinking to myself.

I ran all the way home, passing the familiar signs and posts, moving past other people who had not seen what I had just witnessed. Sasha followed contently. Again, when I got home, my father was not there. It would be rare for Trevor to be home as he was either out gambling, illegally working while claiming benefits or committing some sort of crime. It was quite normal for my dad to be out looking after number one. He taught me well and left me to my own devices. Since Laura had left, I brought myself up. I then fed Sasha and the new puppy. Sabre was so small with his little floppy ears. He had chewed a magazine and pooped on the floor, so I cleaned that up before Trevor came home. I then went upstairs to my bedroom. I had taken over Laura's room since she had left. It was a much bigger bedroom and I could spread out all of my stuff. I often felt that I enjoyed being alone so I had time to think, but sometimes I wonder if it was just because I was so used to it. I thought of those nights when I had felt that deep loneliness and wondered why nobody loved me. I never dwelled long though. Just kept moving. I knew that was the self-esteem talking and the anxiety. Sitting on the bed, I lay back and whispered to myself as if practising a monologue for a play I had no idea about. "The strange feelings... were from a man. A man, that lived in my old house. When I was outside, he would watch me from the window. When I was inside, he was looking for me. Maybe he wasn't bad at all, maybe he was just trying to make a connection with me as he knew I could see and feel him.". I looked at the wall. Staring hard as I thought. I wasn't actually looking at the wall. I was staring through it and into the fabric of time and space. The spirit had reached out to me. Spirits had reached out to me. I had ignored them for so long. Had they been sending me messages? I don't even know if what I felt and thought, were messages. I sensed that there had been signs and hints just to show me the way. To highlight the path, I was meant to be taking.

I was watching a re-enactment from a different time, in my mind. The spot I had been walking over in the woods was where the man had been killed. That smell of the horse. Something had imprinted on that patch of ground and that house. I think the spirit was looking for some sort of acknowledgement, so he wasn't totally forgotten. So that his story was known, and he could move on. This was all part of the 'gift' I was trying to block out. I think he was the man from my house. He must have been trapped there. Trying to get noticed. I had a sudden knowledge that was unexplainable. It was as if I had amnesia and suddenly had a memory return, like it was familiar but completely new. The tall, dark man I had seen in the past and felt around the home, was there. He stood proudly in a field next to what looked like my old house on Agar Road and some horses. My mind went to the photos of the horses I had seen at Agar Road pinned in the shed. Those pictures were old then, so they could have easily been linked. These were visual cues that I should have picked up upon a long time ago. There were children in the background playing. One girl and one boy. What I assumed was a wife, was also present in the picture. The man looked very proud as he patted one of the horses. The children's heads turned to look as if on hinges like swinging stable doors. I watched, invisible to everyone. The sun was so bright for a few seconds and then suddenly turned to rain, heavy rain. This came with a loud clap of thunder and a bright electric bolt of lightning. The field must have been where there were now houses dotted around the property, as I could see similar landmarks that were still visible today like Carn Brea Castle and the tin mines. A voiced beckoned, "Good Day" and all members of the family turned and looked. "You will not get my land!" he shouted, "I have brought my family up here, I was brought up here. We raise our horses and will not be selling. Not over my dead body". The man who was clearly dressed as some sort of businessman, grinned luridly, turned and skulked off down the road saying, "I'm only doing what my father has asked". "Piss off, Roland!" George retorted. "Go tell your sick father he will die long before he gets my land!" The children behind him screamed. As I turned, the children had gone and there was nothing, but a dark sky and a pile of clothes left where they had been. The mother sat in a corner with her head in her hands, sobbing. The children were next to a bush, faces looking deathly and bloated, they were no longer living. Something had happened. Thunder cracked again. Their eyes were hollow and dark. I looked away. I knew what had happened.

Finally, everything began to make sense. The information flowed into my brain, like I was watching a movie. The details so clear and vibrant, that they would stick in my mind forever. The man's name was George. He had a long history of raising horses and breaking them in; some for racing, some for working the land, some for pleasure. The man who George had glared at flashed into my mind and I knew that this was a very greedy man. Son of a land buyer who wanted to destroy the landscape to dig quarries and mine for tin and copper, which were rich in certain areas of the land. I listened and watched intently in this flashback. It seemed that George had been friends with the greedy landowner and when he could not get the land off George, he killed his horses. Whilst doing this and killing them with poison, he had inadvertently poisoned George's children, killing them both. His wife, in a state, then jumped from the local cliff at Hell's Mouth. It transpired that she had fled her home, ran through Tehidy woods at a great pace. People had witnessed her running past them, no-one thought to stop her. She ran so fast, as if fleeing her endless grief. She threw herself from the cliffs into the sea below. Some of the horses were cut up and scattered. Eventually their dead bodies rotted down and became one again with the earth. I was wrong in the idea that the spot was where they met their deaths. Maybe it was the initial place the bodies had been disposed of. I didn't know. I felt the anguish that George had felt at losing his whole family, his business and his love. I felt the agonising collapse inside as he was given the news that his wife's body had been recovered. He couldn't even identify her facially as she had been so battered on the rocks, by the sea. He only saw her wedding ring. It gripped my whole soul with a sense of knowing and total loss of hope. In his grief, George shot himself in the house. In that room downstairs. The room where I saw the shadow figure. Was he the shadow figure? Everything was suddenly beginning to make sense. I had been a witness to a replay of the events that had left the spirit of George trapped.

The imprint it left on the home had attracted darker energy in, as there was definitely something evil there. I didn't feel the same sort of anguish in the house that I did when this man, George, was around. I was more scared when I lived in Agar Road at certain times. I felt that there was something a lot more sinister. I felt like George had been reaching out to me to put the pieces of the jigsaw together, so that I would work out what had happened to him and his family. The darker entity, as I shall call it, could see this and I am sure it wanted to inhabit my body and take over my soul. I believed that George just wanted me to bear witness. For someone to acknowledge what had happened. Some recognition of the terrible events that had happened all those years before. That's what I felt. Maybe this was some form of recognition or justice, I didn't know, but the one thing I did know was that to acknowledge someone's pain, is to share the burden. I knew there was something darker in that house though. I wonder if it ensured that previous occupants couldn't leave. Ones that came after itself and George, but before me. These darker beings were the things that caused my nightmares. That gently pulled at me in the night and screamed ferociously in my ears as I slept. These were the demons that wanted to take my soul. I remember watching Evil Dead, and the demons that came out of the book of the dead would say, "I'll swallow your soul". That's how I felt. After that moment of knowing, I suddenly felt a surge of energy. Like a heavy weight being taken from me . I didn't even know I was carrying it, but it felt like something lifted and dissipated into the air. Released. Free. I didn't understand it, but that's how it happened.

That night I didn't dream. There was such an overload of information from the day, that I simply put on some music. Garbage, "Push It" played followed by, "If You Tolerate This, Your Children Will Be Next" by the Manic Street Preachers. I didn't remember the song after that. I must have drifted off into a deep slumber. I put my head on the pillow and was gone. As I lay in my bed resting, the clouds drew in and the moonlight faded giving way to the dark, heavy and cold rain. The window was opened the tiniest margin and the wind gently lapped at the glass. The rain continued to pour from the black sky. The pavements were sodden, the grass drenched, saturation was inevitable. The clouds hovered ominously in the air, reflecting the dull glow of the orange street lamps. Out of the darkness stepped a silhouette of what I would say was a man in a long, dark outfit. Face blacked out, so there was nothing distinguishable about him at all. No features to see. I felt it was male. Don't ask me how, that's just how it works. My instant thought was the shadow person I had seen in the past. George. No, he had moved on somewhere else. I also felt that. If you sat me down and asked me to vocalise how it feels or what happens when these strange events occur, then it would be extremely difficult for me to put into words. It's all about how things feel and energy. The man just stood there staring up at my window in the dark, eyes transfixed on the spot where I lay. It was as if I was seeing this all in a dream or having some sort of out of body experience. I couldn't tell if it was a memory or if it was real time. There was someone there just standing quietly, watching. Was this a dream or reality? I would never know, but I was aware and indifferent to what I was seeing. The figure continued to look towards me. A flash of lightning lit up the sky. A few seconds later there was a clap of thunder. A storm was coming. The rain poured with such force that the soil was flicking out of the small open patches outside. The figure turned and was gone.

Lanner was a beautiful home for me. I had time to start healing from past traumas. School was pleasant. We would sit in our lessons and chat about EastEnders and what we had seen on the television. We talked about the Top 40 and the fact that Cher had been number one with "Believe" for nearly two months. Again, my music tastes expanded as I was exposed to more and more music. I would listen to The Corrs and sing, "Forgiven, Not Forgotten". These were words I would carry with me through much of my life. I would spend longer in John Oliver's digging through all the CD's and tapes. I found songs by Eagle Eye Cherry, "Save Tonight", The Beautiful South, "Perfect Ten", Sash, featuring Tina Cousins, "Mysterious Times". I used to dance to all my

Spice Girls CD's and tapes down in the lounge. I would shut the shutters and dance for hours. I would also dance to Steps, "One for Sorrow". The CD's had the dance steps inside of it, so I used to copy them. The Spice Girls' dances came from the VHS, 1 Hour of Girl Power. Sometimes I just brought something because I was attracted to the title or name of it. I would often play my CD's in the computer Trevor had purchased after Sid, his friend, had moved out. I used to play "Duke Nukem" with Aqua, "Turn Back Time" and all its remixes playing in the background. I would often be playing Spice Girls, "Too Much", the Soulshock remix and the B-sides, "Walk of life" and "Outer Space Girls", as I played Quake. Trevor would get me to write up fake invoices for him, so that he could do cash in hand work. Smith and Turvill. I was never sure where the Smith came from. Probably some old associate he had fucked over in the past. I never asked, I just did what he asked. Even though I knew what I was doing, he was the one huffing and tutting. Sighing. That would instantly piss me off.

I would also bring up the puppy. I knew my dad would have little input. I would walk the dogs, feed the dogs, brush the dogs. My dad could hardly even remember to feed the two of them when I was out or at my mother's house. Sabre would barge into my tent in the garden to welcome me some mornings. I used to camp in the summer so would always set up my tent and sleep outside. It was a nice escape, waking up to the sounds of birds. Sabre got off his lead once and got kicked in the head by a horse, on the way to Carn Marth, so I often wondered if he was always a bit brain damaged as he seemed to just stay like a puppy, even as he got older. The horses always reminded me of George. Sabre would bark at his own reflection in glass and even jumped through the porch window once or twice. Sasha was much more chilled and dignified. She didn't want all the hustle and bustle. She was happy laying in the lovely garden in the sun. At least she had Sabre for company on cold nights when they weren't allowed in the house and had to stay in the porch. Sometimes I would come home from a weekend at my mother's and he hadn't even cleaned their porch or anything. They were both soaking wet, covered in mud. Poor doggies. I cycled to school most days. It was a good few miles each day. I got the odd lift if my dad was up on time or if it was severe weather or snow. I wouldn't have gotten lifts very often as he didn't work much so never got out of bed. So I spent the rest of that year pretty much playing with friends. Enjoying music. Just being. Just doing. Nothing over the top. I was having a childhood again even if it was brief. As 1999 dawned, I was 15. Growing. Evolving and maturing.

Chapter 6

Another New Life

In this time, the passing of years,
We shed like a snake, losing fears.
And the love we had, helped us survive,
And we will not be mean, just kind

<u>1999</u>

My tape mixes at this stage in my life, were getting bigger and bigger. I would listen to them over and over again on my stereo. On my Walkman as I rode my bike. Everywhere. Even in school, I was disinterested and just listened to my music. I listened to dance songs like, "9pm 'til I come", "Better off Alone", "Back in my Life", "Sweet like Chocolate". I was growing and was also growing in musical taste. So many millions of songs for me to discover and fall in love with. I began to discover Trance music on some of my sister's CD's that she had left at my mum's. Trance took me to another place entirely. "Saltwater" by Chicane was a masterpiece, as well as DJ Sakin and friends, "Protect your Mind". I dreamed of one day playing songs like these to millions of people. Until then, I would dance to them. I loved other pop songs like "Genie in a Bottle",

"Maria", "Pretty Fly for a White guy", "My Love is Your Love" and "It's not Right, But it's Okay". One of my favourites was Sugar Ray, "Every Morning". So many songs, so many artists. Music was like my food. I was still in love with the Spice Girls, but Ginger had left and they had only released "Goodbye" since then, so all had gone quiet. "Kiss Me" by Sixpence None the Richer, was a timeless song that I latched on to. I loved the song mainly because it had an odd band name. It was the B-side "Sad but True", it was edgier and darker. I thoroughly loved it. I was very much attracted to edgier songs with grittier lyrics. I felt like music helped me to digest the trauma of the past and put me at ease with the journey I was on in life. For all this, I still thought I knew it all. I look back at this version of me and know that I knew a lot because of what I'd experienced so young. However, I also knew that I didn't know it all. I wasn't in the right headspace to deal with everything life could and would throw at me.

I was 15 and more aware of the injustice of my childhood. I did look at the people around me and question why they hadn't done more. It would be many, many years before I really understood, but at that moment in time, I was so angry. I was angry that they had let Trevor do that to me, and angry... actually livid, that he could treat a child that way. I couldn't leave though. I had nowhere else to go. I was increasingly more frustrated with my mother and that side of the family, as no-one acknowledged what myself and Laura had gone through. We had to live with the events of our earlier years daily. I was at an age where I could see how relationships worked and felt like my mother had abandoned us. I didn't understand what she had been through at that stage, so I could only feel the injustice of my life at his hands. I, for one, didn't ever go a day without mulling over or trying to process some of what had happened to me when I was younger. I am sure there was even more that we just didn't remember. I had probably repressed years and years of memories. These slowly ebbed out now, as there was no longer any trauma. It was just a constant source of anxiety as I would dream of the things that used to happen. I always wondered how my life would have been if they hadn't treated myself and Laura so badly. I often wondered if I had sought counselling, would that have helped?

It was at this age, I was enjoying myself. I didn't have many close friends, but the ones I had were good, so good. A best friend to last a lifetime. This was how childhood was meant to be. Just being. Careless. Freer than we had ever been. I liked to hope they understood why I behaved the way I did, but who can say. I spent my time playing my CD's on our home computer. I loved buying new music that had the actual videos that I could play on the media player. I would make three or four trips a week to John Oliver's to buy CD's and cassettes. I often had these on in the background while I played Quake and another game called Zombies and Pitchforks – it was very cool. I was beginning to feel more settled now living in Lanner, I had consistent school attendance again and was getting on well. I had less and less fear at home. Trevor was never around, so I just did what I wanted. I rarely heard from Laura. She had escaped and didn't want anything to ruin that. I knew she had been staying at mum's on occasion, as some of her stuff was there – I could completely understand, as she was the only other person who could really understand what my father was like. I still envied her for getting away. Just when things were getting settled and I was moving into my final year of school, Trevor sprang the news.

Suddenly we had to move again. It only seemed like five minutes ago I had been riding home, listening to Bryan Adams and Melanie C, "When you're Gone" and the wonderfully melancholic B-side "Hey baby". Such a great couple of songs. My life was in upheaval again, it was the year before my GCSE's. What was he thinking? I knew he had given my life zero thought. Zero. I should have known that something would happen. My dad had become homeless. I don't know if he had to be made legally homeless to get a council house, but I expected the process to be quick. I thought you would move out of your home and straight into a council house. The really shitty thing was that he could have let me go and live with my mum and stepdad for the time it took, but he wanted to remain selfish and I went nowhere. He didn't want me to escape. He wanted me to go through the same process that he did. The reason we were being made homeless was probably because he hadn't paid the rent on the house or had run up some sort of gambling debts. I often thought I must have done something terrible in a past life to end up living the life I had the way I did. Was it penance or was it to teach me lessons I hadn't learnt before? I don't know, but I felt like it was a huge journey that was just never ending.

Alison had all but disappeared, but I knew when she was around that I would steer clear. I had witnessed true evil in my nightmares and at the face and hands of Alison. I knew that there was more out there and the incident I had experienced in my old home with George, the shadow person, reminded me of this. I felt there were more experiences to have and more spirits to meet with. I didn't understand and felt I needed guidance, but I instinctively thought that will come when it comes. I turned my mind to thoughts of Alison and how evil she was. She was alive. She was the real monster. She was no nightmare; she was part of the cold, harsh reality. I often wondered if there was anything I could do, to ensure she got what was coming to her. My anger simmered beneath the surface for a very long time. I wondered if I would ever be strong enough to tell the rest of the family what she and Trevor had done to me, and if they would even believe me. I thought that people like Trevor and Alison would just get away with everything, never a mark on their conscience. Would karma ever seek them out? I wasn't sure, but I had hoped that time would show them for what they really were.

For eight months, we had to live in a hostel whilst we were waiting for a council flat. It was at this time I discovered the song "Tequila" by Terrorvision and immediately wanted to drink tequila. It was like when I had first heard "I Want to be a Hippy" by Technohead. All I wanted to do was get high like a hippy. I would listen to "Someday" by Sugar Ray and think about one day in the future, when my life had passed me by. I often wondered if I would still be around that far in the future. It would lead me to thoughts like why I was still alive . I wasn't suicidal or anything, but I did often think

that it would have been easier to not be around.
I wouldn't have had to have gone through the events
I did, or deal with the aftermath. Just fade out of
existence. I wanted to live, however this was my life and
I didn't want to give it up. I suffered some of my
darkest moments in that hostel. Every time I left, I had
to put on a front that everything was fine. It wasn't,
I was trying my best. I was trying very hard. I had to
share one room with my father. This had a severe
impact on me. It was one room for the two of us to live
in. A bedsit. I don't even know how I got all my
schoolwork done there. It was big enough for two single
beds, a little chest of drawers and a chair that was
in front of the TV that Trevor had brought with him.
I literally had no possessions of my own as all my stuff
had gone into storage.

I was forced into a dark hole where I couldn't escape.
I felt trapped in this room, in the loud hostel where I
even had to share a bathroom with other families. It was
a period where I spent as much of the daylight hours
outside as I could, and in the evenings, I wasted the time
with my friends; drinking, smoking cannabis and trying
to laugh about the terrible situation I found myself in.
None of this was my fault, I kept telling myself. In the
days of secondary school, it was hard to keep up
appearances as all the other kids had the latest gadgets,
clothes and nice houses, while I was in a one-roomed
bedsit with my unsettling father, in this hostel. I didn't
tell anyone from school about this. A couple of times
friends had asked if they had seen me leaving that place
and I made an excuse that I was meeting someone there.
I don't know if they believed me. I was ashamed and

embarrassed. The doors were shut and locked at a certain time, so sometimes I never even got back into the building. Then there were the really drunk, violent guys in the hallway or outside smoking fags and shouting. It really unnerved me. I didn't like confrontation, and this just brought me down further. The poor dogs were stuck in an animal shed over on my dad's friend's farm. They spent so many months locked away up there and I don't know how often my dad let them out. Poor old Sasha was aging and it wasn't the most comfortable life for her in there. Like me, she had had a rough life. I prayed for adulthood to hurry up and come, so that I didn't have to deal with the terrible Trevor anymore. I dreamt of escape and finding love in a hopeless place. I spent so many moments during those eight months, in total despair. Stuck on that bed, crippled with anxiety and dread. I could not escape him. One room, shut in most of the time. He was selfish and wouldn't let me go and stay with my mother. He knew deep down if I left, I would never come back. I should have gone and never returned. Hindsight is a beautiful thing.

As my most formative years began to end at the age of nearly 16, Trevor and I finally moved into a council flat. At first, I was very unhappy with this as it had two bedrooms, stairs straight up into the flat, a lounge, kitchen and very small bathroom. There was a lot less room than I was used to, but as soon as I unpacked all my items, I felt a lot better. I began to be able to breathe again. I had my own space. It wasn't as big as the houses we had previously had, and the neighbours were rough, but I was grateful to have a roof over my head again. It was just nice to have my own space and home. When we moved in, I found a small box of tapes in the attic.

There were lots of Oasis songs on them, which I began to love. I played them over and over, as I did with all the other music I found. I often wondered who had bequeathed them to me. What they were like. I finally had my own bedroom again, my own possessions back. My own space. It was like a little piece of heaven. When I looked out of my bedroom window, I could see directly over the top of all the houses, up across the Redruth School fields and I had an amazing view straight across to Carn Brea where the castle and monument stood. Sunsets were amazing from there. I did have a lot of colour in my life all of a sudden.

3 Vorfield Close

As I walked around Redruth with my friends, I looked at the old Brewery, where we used to play as kids. It had been turned into a massive Tesco supermarket. I looked back on these memories fondly and tried to recall what had happened to all the kids I had grown up with and grown apart from. Hannah and I would go down to the Tesco on our lunchbreaks and get donuts. Sometimes we would wander into town, sharing a headphone and get food from there. We would sometimes get things pierced on our lunchbreaks, just to see how much it hurt. I remember getting my first tattoo at 16, a Chinese symbol. I passed out when I left the shop, as I was hungover from the night before. The memory of the night before was very blurry, but I remember being in my friend James's attic doing a Ouija board. The main thing I remembered was that apparently my great granddad came through and the words that repeated over and over were, "Send the letter, send the letter". It just repeated and repeated and repeated. I didn't know what that meant. I could send a letter to anyone. I thought someone was pushing the glass and just trying to wind me up. We would sneak into under-18's at Twilight Zone up the road to get drunk and dance away to songs like "Zombie Nation" by Kerncraft 400, Tukan, "Light a Rainbow", Lost Witness, "7 Colours", Fragma, "Toca's Miracle", Mojo, "Lady, Hear Me", Chicane, "Don't give up". I remember my first experience with harder drugs, dancing to the songs here. I tried a quarter of an Ecstasy tablet. I was too afraid to try more. I wanted to experiment, I was young. I never tried anything too bad, but I just wanted to see how it felt. It felt like ultimate escapism from my life. I was feeling nothing and everything all at once. I was weightless and time would stand still as the songs would pass. We would sweat away as we danced for hours to DJ Luck and MC Neat, "With a Little bit of Luck" and Artful Dodger, "Moving too Fast". It was about this time I got my first Trance Nation CD's. I was heavily into experimenting and skiving school again at this point. I was rebelling really but also without boundaries, I thought I could do what I wanted. We would sleep at the beach. When I came home, I would crash out hard.

I remember that one night, I had a dream where I was wandering the hallways of my school. Everything was empty. There was not another person there to be seen. The white walls gleamed and the wooden floors patterned and zigzagged away from me, reaching further and further down the spectral corridor. I headed past the old canteen to my right and heard the faint cluttering of cutlery in the distance. I heard the jostling of the large metallic dishes that the food was served in, and remembered how I had felt in infant school when they brought out the cheesy swirls or the pink semolina. Happy memories of contentment and food. I noticed that most of my good memories in life revolved around what I was eating at the time or what I had planned to eat. I chuckled to myself. Everything was quiet as I roamed the halls. I knew that I had no reason to be there, but I was there nonetheless. I knew I was dreaming, as I had never been in a school completely emptied. Throughout all of this, I remained asleep. Lucid dreaming was becoming fairly normal to me. I was aware I was dreaming, but I had no way of controlling any aspect of the dreams. I could never quite get to the point where I could control anything. A loud ring filled the air as the school bell suddenly went off. No children came from the empty classrooms, no teachers on patrol during the breaktimes. It was very eerie to hear this alarm, but there be no response to it. I felt as if the people had been removed. Taken away from me and everyone else. Forcibly removed. The classroom door next to me opened, but nothing came out. I entered this door hesitantly and found myself in the old art room where I had made pottery figures years before, that had been fired in the kiln. As I opened the kiln door to look inside, my ears pricked and I turned around. I heard a giggle. I knew the giggle. It was the IT clown from the Stephen King film I had seen years before. It petrified me every time it appeared. As I took a deep breath and looked down at my feet, I was transported to another place.

A second later, I was in a night club. I walked through the crowd of people who danced in silence and stared at a table in the far-left hand corner with a piece of paper on it. The paper was unreadable to me, but I knew it was a letter of some sort. I glanced down at the letter and all I could make out at the end was my own name. Was it something I had written? It seemed awfully strange and without giving it a second thought, I began to dance with the others as Delirium, "Silence" began to play. I melted away into the music. As I danced into the beat, people kept on pointing at the letter on the table. "Send it", I heard faint voices whisper.

"Send the letter…", it was clear, but I didn't understand it. Letters were sent extremely often, this was before the world went email mad. I awoke with a slight sense of fear, but when I processed the dream, it turned to a sense of peace. I couldn't understand that feeling or how I came to that decision. Again, it was just some sort of knowing. It was then that I knew I had taken myself out of the scary situation in my dream. I had lucid dreamed.

2000

As I approached and passed my GCSE's, I began fucking up in my own way. I did pass all my exams, but I was so drunk or high that I don't really know how I did it. I guess I was very intelligent. I was at an age where I was processing all that happened to me and starting to see it with adult eyes. I think that is why it was so traumatic. Things that I had ignored for years, were coming to the surface. I just didn't want people around me. I wanted to be alone to deal with it all. I often thought, and still sometimes think, that if I had had a different father, then maybe I'd have had a better upbringing and I'd have made a lot more of my life. People say you can't blame everything on your parents, but I certainly blamed mine. I then passed into the first and second year of A-Levels. The only real work I did for two years of A-Levels was in English. I really enjoyed "The Handmaid's Tale" and "A Clockwork Orange". They were both very dark and dystopian. Deep and meaningful. I was stoned nearly all the time and took very little in, I am sure. I would often skive and had a very poor attendance over those two years. I preferred to stay at home and watch programs like Hope and Faith, and Greenclaws. I was processing the whole mishap of my childhood. At the time, I thought I was having a whale of a time, but in hindsight I can see how deeply unhappy I was. I had discovered drugs in a big way and these took me away to another place. I tried various things, but I often smoked cannabis. I would invite my friends around and we would listen to hip hop; Tupac, Eminem, Dr Dre and then get high and watch Buffy the Vampire Slayer. I had an affinity with the Slayer. She was put upon the earth and forced into battling with darkness – that's how I saw it, anyway. Life was a big fight and week after week this show helped me through, the same way music had.

Hannah and I hung out. We would get drunk and get a Chinese takeaway most Saturdays and watch Charmed and other shows. Her mum always thought it was me being the bad influence, sending her home drunk. We had some extremely funny times. When I had lived elsewhere and was a few years younger, I used to just go on trips and occupy my mind that way. The way with smoking was that I'd forget everything that had ever happened to me. I was in a state of what I thought was equilibrium and grace. I thought that because I didn't feel anything, then everything was all right. It wasn't. I was naïve to think that at the time. I am sure deep down I knew, but was in denial. I was dealing with my childhood issues. The feelings about my sexuality, myself. It was all so much. I didn't know it then, but I was such a mess. High functioning and doing a lot of what I had to do, but in private I was a recluse. I didn't want to go out. I just wanted to get off my face and listen to music. I felt the music much more deeply when I was mellowed. I would listen to everything, including "Stan" by Eminem, "Always on Time" by Ja Rule, "Wherever you Go" by The Calling, and DB Boulevard, "Another Point of View". I even wrote down all the lyrics to some songs and used to practice them over and over again. "Ride Wid Me", by Nelly was a song that my friends and I loved, as we used to dream of going out, driving and smoking. I guess that's what you did as you got older. I felt like I didn't fit into the social norms, so I followed what everyone else did. I had my own obsessions, music and such, but in terms of going out, I followed. I was engrossed more and more in Dance and Trance songs such as Riva, "Who do you Love?", Fragma, "You are Alive", Basement Jaxx, "Romeo". "Let it all go!" the song chanted.

I also began to get more into hip hop and rap. I guess as we were smoking cannabis, we should have been more gangster. I soon found that the music was exceptional, but also the lyrics and stories were extremely deep. I didn't like raps all about bitches and hoes, but Tupac and Eminem would tell stories. That spoke to me so much more. The Spooks, "The Things I've Seen", was such a good track that I had on auto repeat. I would sing my heart out to Oasis songs like "Little by Little" and ironically, "Stop crying your Heart Out". I seemed to experience music on a cellular level. It seeped into my very essence and I felt as if it was healing me with the experience and words. Soul food.

Living with my father, I knew the potential of what he could do, but it had been a long time since anything like that had happened. I spent my days smoking weed, getting high, watching my favourite shows and hanging out with friends. My best friend, Hannah was a constant source of comfort and we went everywhere together. I experimented with my friends with magic mushrooms and some LSD. When I was on magic mushrooms, I thought that I was growing one minute and shrinking the next. I even hallucinated that there was a wasp in my mouth, which made me freak out. I recalled how something had hit me in the head earlier in the day at home and I shrugged it off. As soon as I saw the wasp on the windowsill, I realised that was what had hit me in the head earlier. Because my senses were so heightened, the thought was immediate, and I imagined that it had flown straight into my mouth. I was in the corner of my room, mere feet from my father saying, "It's in my mouth, it's in my mouth.".

We all played a card game called Shithead, which I loved – then and all of a sudden, the cards lost all meaning to me and I turned to my friends, questioning, "What do I do with these?" My friends went around the corner to the shop and I went on a magical trip, and when they returned, I was found camping in my bedroom. I had shifted all the furniture to one end of the room and set up my tent at the other, listening to vocal Trance songs like, "Stay With Me" by Angelic and "Pretty Green Eyes" by Ultrabeat. I was transported to a serene, heavenly place. The mixture of music and drugs was exquisite and removed me further from the pain I had felt all my life. All the memories that I was plagued with daily.

I wasn't afraid of my father anymore, but I didn't forget. I was bigger than him now and possibly stronger, physically. I had come to realise that everything that had happened was down to Alison and her sick and twisted nature. However, deep inside I was still angry at my father for going along with it all, plus he was the one who actually dished out the punishments. So why shouldn't I be angry at him? He was a bitter, horrible man who only manipulated people to get what he wanted. I "Eukkked" to myself every time he returned home or even spoke to me. It was also at this point that I stopped talking to all the rest of my family. I had felt so abandoned by them, that I didn't want any contact. I was trying to come to terms with being gay and the abuse. I just felt like I didn't want anyone around. I didn't want to see them, as it was a constant reminder that no one stopped it and that no-one was talking about what had happened. At the same time, I felt so bad about myself that I felt isolated and that I didn't deserve their time or affection, as I couldn't tell them who I was. I remember coming out briefly to my mother and her response wasn't as positive as I had hoped for, so I knew I would never be able to come out to my father. He would not like the idea of having a gay son. So, I told him nothing. I guess I'd always known deep down that I was gay, but as far as I was concerned it was a part of life that was private and didn't need talking about. Maybe if I had had a better upbringing and a more open and caring parent, I'd have felt safer and better about coming out. I remembered what my father had said years ago about that EastEnders gay kiss, so I knew he was deeply homophobic. I sometimes wondered if that's why Trevor had always been so hard on me, trying to man me up or something. It reminded me of a trip to Butlins where I cried the whole time as he forced me to play football, and I really didn't want to. Trevor Turvill could not have a gay son. Imagine what people would say! I spent most of this time just getting high and listening to a lot of music. So much to even remember, from Pink Floyd to Dido, and Kosheen.

As 2003 approached, I had somehow got into college. I had about 34% attendance for my A-Levels over two years, which was appalling, but somehow scraped into college nearby. I suddenly realised the dream I had had about the empty school was what was happening to me. Everyone who had been at school with me all the way along and stayed on in sixth form with me, were now leaving. We were all going our own ways. Though I was growing and I was feeling happier as an adult, I still carried the burden of my abuse. I look back at that time and realise how lost I really was. What a horrible foggy world I lived in. I was having the time of my life, but at the same time I was deeply out of control. Fully off the rails and just detonating. I wasn't having many experiences at this point. I wondered if it was because I had hazed my mind with booze and drugs. I read a book about drugs actually expanding the mind, so I did wonder. I just felt like I wasn't in the right place to have visitations. Plus, where I lived wasn't haunted. It was comfortable. Most of my experiences came when I was out of the house. I could always do what I wanted. I got the odd inkling that something wasn't right, but generally there was nothing. I studied Animal Science, as I was interested in the psychology of animal behaviour. I also began to work as a Support Worker in a local house. It was a very big property with about 15 bedrooms, a communal lounge and downstairs in the basement was the huge kitchen with a huge oven in a massive, old fireplace. This was my first proper job and I was a little scared at times, but it was fun. I enjoyed it. This room led out of the back of the house and into a courtyard. I lived nearby, so it was very easy to walk there. It was there that I began to have the odd sense again. One night, I even saw a man who I thought was a resident go into the washroom. This room had no way out and it was very dark. I walked in there and said, "What are you doing?". As I walked in there, the room was empty and completely dark.

I had these feelings in this house. It turned out it was an old hospital and many babies were born there, so it could have been anything. Any sort of spirit or energy. There could have been stillborn's or babies that didn't survive after birth. Mothers may have died in childbirth. All sorts of energy could have leeched into the brickwork over the years. I began to see Richie at this time. The one. The love of my life. But it wasn't meant to be. I think I was too emotionally damaged at that age and he was as well. We stuck it out for a good long while though. It was also here that I met another one of my best friends, Joanna Smith. We got to talking one day and I said that some neighbours had told me that the last occupant had died in the bathroom. She told me that she had seen my name and address on some paperwork in the office and knew that she had actually lived in the flat before me. So it transpired that she had moved out for the place to be redecorated, but had never actually moved back and the Oasis tapes that I had found in the attic and listened to, were hers. Now that couldn't have been a coincidence. We have been best friends ever since. Smith and Turvill. That's why even then when I used to type out Trevor's invoices for him, Smith and Turvill was everywhere. Hints to the future from the past. We have been through so much together over the years and I am thankful for her every day. She stuck around when I came out to my straight friends. They disowned me. I was very sad about that as I wasn't ready to come out to them. It should have been my choice, when I felt comfortable. In all honesty, they proved me right as they all made assumptions that if I was gay, I would try it on with them. That couldn't have been further from the truth. They were my friends. One of my friends did drunkenly throw himself at me and we did whatever, but after that I barely saw him again. It was a great shame. All I ever asked for was understanding and acceptance. That was all I wanted to say on that side of my life, as it isn't a story about that. I am who I am.

I spent a lot of time with Joanna. We would drive around and pick her kids up from school singing the Killers songs, Kaiser Chiefs and Greenday at the top of our lungs. We would go on adventures. We would avidly watch "Takeshi's Castle" and we started to watch a program called "Most Haunted." Now that was a program that opened my imagination. Whether it was real or not, I felt that it was something I wanted to do. I wanted to explore the unknown. It was about this time I got very interested in ghostly, paranormal, spiritual stuff again. I watched a lot of shows on television. Most Haunted was a favourite. It was creepy, but also very funny. I liked the mixture of the history, the actual hunt and the mediums explanations of events. I spent most of my time through these couple of years seeing my friends, seeing my boyfriend. Living life. It could have been a hell of a lot better, but I was trying my best. I think I was at an age where I knew everything that had happened to me and who was at fault, and I couldn't find any way out of the memories. I was anxious. I was emotional. All I wanted was someone, so I threw myself at anyone who showed an interest. I was trying to fill a void.

My dad left me to do whatever I wanted. I was really an emotional mess. I learnt to drive, which took a while as I was always so stoned. When I eventually passed, it wasn't long before I crashed my first car. It was at this stage, Richie became a bit of a prick. He broke up with me because I had crashed the car that he had given me. He didn't ask how I was or anything. It was all about his car, his object. That said a lot to me. We did get back together after a while, but it was a bit of a blow just after a car accident. However, in the moment when the crash happened, I heard a voice somewhere inside that said, "Don't worry, it will be all fine". And it was. The only injury I had was from a CD flying across the car and hitting me in the face. My father came to pick me up as the police were there and I was in shook, and he actually laughed. I remember that. It was just a snigger, but I thought, well, fuck you. Just fuck you for everything. I had so much hatred for my father at this stage, but I was in no fit state to do anything about it. I couldn't move out, as I spent all my time working or trying to get out of my head. I hated the way my father charmed people, like a narcissist, manipulating and exploiting them. However, he seemed to stay out of my way, which I liked. He let me just smoke and whatever in my bedroom, so I had it easy. I didn't have to pay any rent. I think I told him once when I came home hammered, that he owed me and should pay for me to work things out in my own time. He never disagreed. Trevor had no conscience or reason in him, so not much got through. If it did, he certainly didn't show it. He never showed an ounce of remorse.

When Trevor was out at work, I would go to college and meet with my friends. I'd go driving with Hannah and exploring random, cool places. I enjoyed a quiet life. There came a day when Trevor, now approaching 60, sized up to me over something really menial, like the dog had shit in the kitchen or something. I just lost the plot and as he raised a fist to me; I cried at him, "What are you going to do, hit me like when I was a child?". This seemed to shock and stop Trevor, but he never apologised or showed any remorse for his actions, then or for when I was younger. Trevor knew deep down he and Alison were to blame. He knew. He would just never say it.

I told Richie about what had happened to me and he didn't really seem to believe it. Well who would believe? A lot of it was pretty farfetched, but it did happen. I was still reeling. It was clearly taking a very long time for me to deal and come to terms with it all. Although we were together, it was always very strained. I was often angry as Richie appeared quite immature and restrictive in his thoughts. He wasn't open to change, and me, well, I was incensed almost all the time. I was young and immature. I had been livid for a long time. It had eaten me up. I wasn't violent like my father, but my temper was very quick to fray. I would storm off or lose my rag over the smallest thing. I spent a long time like that. There were also very good times between all of this, but with adolescence came arguing, frustration. But also, such joy. Without the proper hassles of adulthood, that in-between gap when you can still almost do what you want, when you want, without having to get up to work every day or pay all the bills and do the shopping. When you are, just for a short time, totally free. I always knew that this period should have been longer for me, but I didn't have a childhood when I was small.

One summer evening in 2004, I was picked up by Richie. I had reached the ripe old age of 19 and we went for a holiday in Cumbria. It was a beautiful time. I recount how the sun shone so brightly; the mountains were amazing. We visited as many of the small towns as we could, and laughed as a swan went for our chips on

Lake Windermere. I remembered that it was so hot one day and that so many green flies had hatched, that we couldn't leave the tent. The field was a thick green fog of invertebrates. How we laughed one evening when something got into the tent and ran off with my donuts, I think it was a fox or a badger, but we both nearly excreted in our pants at the time. Colliford Lake was beautiful, where the Bluebird crashed many years before. I realised at this time, that although I was damaged, I could still have a life and that this life was better than what I had previously experienced. There was love here between us two. There was nothing to explain, no-one to hide from or avoid. It was Andrew and Richie. Us. That trip was amazing. The soundtrack of my life at the time was Snow Patrol. A perfect album for a wonderful time. Halfway between healing and hurting. There was a lot of hope and optimism. We listened to dance music together. We used to turn the bass up loud as the hard house beats would kick in, "Happiness seems to be loneliness... and loneliness killed my world...".

I used to listen to Vanessa Carlton, "A Thousand Miles" whenever I was going to see him. He introduced me to Roxy Music, "More Than This", which has become one of my favourite songs. I have a lot of favourite songs. Anyone who knows me, would say that I pretty much say it about every song I listen to. A song for every moment and a song for every mood. When we returned to Cornwall, I had an anxiety dream. I was dreaming about the shadow figure again at Agar Road. All the past energies I had felt and strange things I had seen. They sort of came at me all at once. I often guessed what people were going to say before they said it. Or I would think of someone and they would suddenly ring me. Too many little things, than when you pieced them together, were so obvious. Just little coincidences that I didn't really pay any attention to all of the time. I didn't know if it was the house or a demon reaching out to me on a weird psychic level, but every time I had an odd dream, I was always at the house or it was about that house. I didn't know, but the older I got, the more I instinctively just knew that I was right about these things. There was some knowledge or information presented at to me at times when it was required. Just when it was needed. I would go to people's houses and say, "There's a little girl on the stairs", and people would wonder how I knew when they showed me old clippings. Joanna and I continued to avidly watch Most Haunted and began to do a few ghost hunts of our own. We went to various woods, such as Kennal Vale, and would later do full nights at Pengersick Castle and other places. It was like I was obsessed. Joanna had a medium come to her house one evening and they told me that I would shy away from it, but at the same time I was well into it and would want to know more. At that stage, I didn't want to know more. I was still closing myself off to things that happened, even though it felt natural when they did. The older I got, the more I understood it. I understood death, but I didn't like it and I wasn't sure if I wanted to delve too far into it. I always had a view of death that it was something to be afraid of. An ending of something. Life. At that time Sasha had lost the use of her back legs, as some German Shepherds do, and she had to be put to sleep. I was very upset by this. I always felt closer to animals than people, and losing Sasha was like losing a friend. She was severely missed. It was at this point, my dad had decided to get another dog so that Sabre wasn't on his own. He brought home a little Labrador cross that looked a bit like a reverse Dalmatian. I named him Snoop or Snoop D O Double-G, I used to call him after the rapper. Unfortunately, we didn't have him for very long as he got run over as a puppy. I told my father that the fence wasn't suitable and that he would get out, and on to the road. My dad clearly knew better and seemed very surprised when the dog jumped the fence and ran away. After he had escaped the garden, he must have run onto the A30, which was not very far away at all. I was out of my mind looking for him. It was a day later that the local men from the council came and knocked on the door. They presented me with a large envelope that contained his bloody collar. He had been run over. I think it was bad, as they said they had to dispose of the body. Poor little puppy. It wasn't long after this that I began to feel the odd sensations I had grown up with. I felt there was something with me at home. Nothing horrible, but just something, someone there. I would often say to my friend that I thought it was Snoop who was visiting me, as I would see something black and low out of the corner of my eye. It wasn't a solid black shape, more like a blur. It appeared to be down low to the ground, like a dog sort of height. I would often see it whilst I was hoovering or in my bedroom. As if the dog had come up the stairs and was peering around the corner into my bedroom. One day I said to my friend, "That is my dog Snoop", and I said into the air, "I see you Snoop". As soon as I acknowledged him, I never saw him again. I loved Snoop, as did Sabre. I really wanted to say, "I told you so" to my dad for not sorting the fencing out, but I bit my tongue. There was a lot of tongue biting going on.

I used to sneak Richie in when Trevor was out. I even snuck him into Tremorvah, where I worked. That was very dodgy, but it was fun. My dad would have killed us both if he knew about our relationship. We had a couple of close calls. I'm sure my dad must have known what was going on, but nothing was ever said. That was like the theme of all of our lives, keep everything under wraps. Don't say a word. I tried to keep it discreet, but sometimes it was obvious what we had been doing. I just didn't have any feeling or respect for him to even want to tell him. I felt like my father was someone with whom I lodged with and he deserved no explanation of who I was and where I would be going. I did question whether to tell him a couple of times, but soon decided against it as I always had the fear of him kicking me out. Though I was all he had left of his family. I did wonder if me being the only one left, would stop him from saying or doing horrible things. However, I knew Trevor, he had form, so I didn't put anything past him. He treated everyone better than his own family.

Sometimes when I was home alone, the phone would ring. As soon as I said, "Hello", the line would go dead. I always assumed it was Alison. She clearly couldn't bear to speak to me, which was fine. I knew my dad still saw her, as he occasionally said he was going out with her for the day. I hadn't seen her at the flat, but then I wasn't there a lot of the time. I had work, friends and my life to be getting on with, so was often out. I don't even know how often Alison came around anymore. One time I remember her saying, "Is your father there?". I'd reply with, "No, he's out shagging his new girlfriend". I'm sure she could hear the malice in my voice. I began to realise something. Why did I ever fear her? I was becoming a grown man. I had no need to fear her anymore. It had been a long time coming. "I know we haven't had the best relationship...", she piped in. All I could ever say was, "Oh, what the fuck? Fuck off, Alison.".

Even the parrot that my dad had brought would mimic the phone ringing and then say, "Hello" in my dad's voice, and also, "Then fuck off, you fucking bitch". Lovely. I revelled in it when I heard anything like that. The parrot was called Squeak, he was an African Grey and a cheeky little character. He had a wonderful personality. I remember my dad telling Hannah he was friendly and then as Hannah approached, the parrot squawked and dug his claws into my dad's head. We used to laugh about that a lot. The parrot also used to call the dogs. He would say, "Come on Sabre, come on". Then when the dog approached, he would shout in my dad's tone, "Go and lay down!", the poor dog didn't know where to put himself. Sometimes Squeak would start chattering away in the middle of the night and I always thought it was a ghost. He would do a cackle and hiss and then shout some sort of expletive. Another animal my dad had taught well.

I began to take more notice of mediums on the television and read a lot more books on the subject. I liked the way that some mediums said they were given information or saw pictures in their minds that linked to certain things. That's how I felt I worked. Maybe there was some sort of mediumistic ability. I tried to get Richie interested in some ghost hunting, but he was always a sceptic. When I told him about things I had experienced, he didn't really believe me, but he went along with it anyway. One night we went into Richie's place of work and did a ghost hunt of our own. I had watched Most Haunted so many times that I knew what to do. I fashioned my own Ouija board out of pieces of paper and a glass I had pinched from Trevor's cabinet. It was a massive empty mansion. Proper haunted house style. We went through as many rooms as we could. I wanted to inspect and investigate every inch of the house that I could. "So, you really believe in all this crap!" said Richie. "SHHHH" I snapped, "seriously, we are here to see if there is anything". We went down quietly into the cellar and turned off the lights. Richie stood close by. "Did you hear that?" said Richie. "What?". "Listen…" Richie shushed.

"It could be a rat."

"SHHH, listen!"

"I don't want to get bitten by a big, fat rat," I squealed. "I bit you," Richie smiled at me. This seemed to alleviate the tense atmosphere for a few seconds. It was moments like that that made everything I had been through more acceptable. Just for sheer moments when I was with someone who didn't question or judge me or want anything other than me. To just be together and have fun. Enjoy the time we were having and not looking for something else. That is probably what being content is all about.

"Jokes aside. This is dumb now in a cellar in the middle of the night. No-one knows we are here, we could both be murdered and that would be that.".

There was an odd scraping noise, but it could have been the door to the cellar gently scraping as it was old wood and looked pretty unsteady on its hinges. I heard a strange breathing. It wasn't either of us.

"Right I am out of here, this is ridiculous!" I shouted in a frightened tone. I heard the breath again and fled out of the cellar, forgetting that it had a low entrance. I bashed my skull on the low granite, but still carried on, wincing and rubbing the impact spot. Richie just laughed, so I thought I'd get my own back. We both took a few photos and I even had one with an orb in it from the attic, but Richie remained sceptical. I think he needed to see a full-blown apparition that would say, "Boo" to him. To play a joke on him, I opened a cupboard door as we went by and moved some items quickly. Upon our return to that spot, Richie noticed the door open and freaked out. He started crying and ran from the building. I never told him of this, but I chuckled about it for a very long time. I had a cheeky trickster side too. I was kind of happy, but at the same time empty. When it was good between us, it was good. When it was bad, it was terrible.

I still hadn't spoken to my most of my family for a couple of years. My mum had tried to get in touch and I just didn't want the contact. I wasn't in a place emotionally to deal with anything, so I pushed them all away. All of my family. I just wanted to get wasted. I'd dropped out of college and just did my support work, which I loved. I loved the way that Richie made me feel as well. Of course, there were some terrible times, but it was mainly good. A learning curve. Just hanging out under the stars. We even spent one New Year's Eve parked down near St. Michael's Mount in a van. We lined it with candles and saw the new year in. That was living. I was free. Maybe I was a bit young and extremely immature and things didn't pan out the way they could have, but I was loved. I look back and think that I didn't have all the skills to have a proper relationship. I wasn't brought up to respect anyone, so it was hard for me to learn all these skills. I always knew what I wanted to do and say, but I found it hard to express myself adequality. I also think that as I had been starved of love as a child, that I was often clingy and needy. I eventually learnt that no-one likes that. Even I didn't when people did it to me. Richie and I would spend hours just driving around in the car. Just chilling, hanging out and listening to music. He showed me new music and I did the same. We would often do a trip down to Lands' End and play songs like, Roger Sanchez, "Another chance", Fragma, "Every Time you Need Me", DJ Sammy, "The Boys of Summer" and "The Opera Song" by Jurgen Vries. So many different songs, different remixes. I adored music, always have and always will.

I recalled how Richie had once told me that he loved me for everything I had been through, all that I had become, despite it. Beautiful words from a beautiful person. I always felt that this was my soulmate, and that if times or we had been different in thought and maturity, then we would have lasted. That was my one big love and it was grand. It didn't last, but I look back on it with such a fondness and happy warm fuzzy feelings. Young love is the best. It was exquisite. There were moments when I felt so annoyed with him, but when I look back with hindsight, they were the best times of my life. That's what I carry through my life. All those moments when I was out and proud with him. I had no doubts or troubles. Everything seemed to melt away when we were together. I was just one of those things that happened. We parted our ways. We nearly got back together. Then it was all over again. There was too much back and forth, and in the end, I had to just let go. Maybe it was wrong place, wrong time, but right person. Who can say? All I know is I was happy to have experienced that feeling and emotion then, so that in the years that have since passed, I can look back on it, revisit it and smile. I feel that neither of us were equipped to deal with each other long term. We both had our damage that we were working through. He was definitely the one. I see that. I enjoyed it all at the time, but with age I feel like I could have appreciated it and him more. It was a truly wonderful time. If I had to die tomorrow, I'd at least know I experienced that. When we departed, it was me and my friends again, "It's a brave new world that we live in.".

Chapter 7

Out of the blue, into the fire

With age comes wisdom,
But with wisdom, comes age,
See the beauty of the fire
Feel the burning of the rage

Time passed so quickly, I noticed this more as I got older, to the age of 22. There were subtle events that had happened and the dark entity that had stood under the streetlight many years before, made the odd appearance. Sometimes it stood silently in the background. I never saw it, but it was there all the same. I didn't really think of that at that point. I didn't even notice when the dark entity stood outside my home, just silently watching. As if checking upon where I was. I never knew anything of this. It never looked for interaction or recognition. It never attempted to come inside. It was almost as if it was looking over me. I had forgotten about a lot of things due to mentally blocking and the passage of time, but I was coming through it. I was still strong. I had still survived, even though I spent a few years struggling. I very nearly gave up once and had written letters to everyone. I then took a massive overdose, but woke up the next day fine. I didn't want to die. It was just an extreme reaction to a culmination of years of circumstance. It didn't work anyway so I took it as a hint that it wasn't my time. I think back to that time in my life and am glad I survived because I have experienced so much since then and have been so blessed in many, many ways. I still tried and did enjoy a lot of this period of my life. I had believed in fate for a while and I did think if it was meant to be with Richie or whoever, then it would have been or would be. I was patient. I wasn't looking for anything. At that moment in time, I was just like the song by Jurgen Vries called Wilderness; "Where am I now? I am looking but can't see ahead... I'm falling away, I am lost in the wilderness. I'm falling away on the wings of a prayer, I'm travelling through, riding high into paradise and all I can see is wilderness.".

I was still dealing with the childhood trauma that had caused me to continue experimenting with drugs, such as LSD and Ecstasy. I danced so hard in the night clubs. Arm in the air, grooving to the music, in an ecstasy of feelings, chills and waves. The hard house trance released something in my soul. Uplifting vocal, they called it. It took me to another place. Somewhere I got lost in the music, further than I had ever been. Trance Nation Electric remixes, Basement Jaxx, "Goodluck", "Luminary" by Amsterdam, the Super 8 Remix and Bedrock, "Heaven Sent" remix. I lived for music. I really wanted to learn guitar. I had always wanted to learn guitar. I just thought at the time it would never happen. It was too complicated, I'd never be able to do it. Richie had even brought me one, but I kept giving up when I couldn't play the chords. Music had been and was always there for me. It was there when I was down or alone, or scared and happy, I always had music. I could escape in it. Get lost in it. Plus, everyone knows music is soul food. Nourishing. I had been introduced to new music by various people over the years and I always strived to find new music. I knew that this was important to me.

"People who can show you new music are important to have", I always used to exclaim. I really enjoyed introducing people to other music as well. I would visit a local gay club. The whole lifestyle and scene never really appealed to me, but it was somewhere I felt I had to go and try to find someone. All I wanted was to find someone who I could meet up with and do all the relationship things with, but then when I wanted to dance, just let me dance. I felt a lot of people's emotions and always picked up on their feelings. Some said it was an empathic gift. This left me feeling very tired. Some people's energies would just sap the life from me. I would need a lot of alone time just to recharge and refuel. I was soon realising why I spent so much time alone. It wasn't just because of what had happened to me when I was younger. It was partly to do with that, but if I was some sort of empath then it meant that just being around other people was tiring. Filtering through all their emotions as well was knackering. It was constant and I never really knew how to shut it off then.

2006

By 2006, I was working full-time and experiencing my young adulthood. I did the usual things, went out clubbing, went to parties etcetera. I should have done a lot more, but I was still quite introverted and anxiety would often stop me going out. I still spent a lot of time alone in my room doing whatever I did. Healing. Recharging. I was getting a bit older and went through other relationships. I moved in with the next partner. I lived with him for about a year, even moved all the way to Trewellard, a beautiful village near the tip of the county, but it didn't work out. I think we were both so damaged and he was very volatile. I would go and see live bands with Hannah and my friends. We saw Amy Winehouse in 2007, Juliette Lewis and the Licks, and KT Tunstall in 2008. I saw Ash with my friend Joanna. We all loved live music. It was what I lived for. I went from listening to lots of music alone, to going to concerts. It was like everybody there was bonded by the music. It was like group therapy. I was enjoying my life at last. When I lived at Trewellard down at Pendeen, it was amazing. It was right near the sea. It was old mining country. There were ghost stories, soaring moors, deep coves and hidden beaches. There were dilapidated ruins and old mine buildings and cliffs that sailed high above the water below. I would have stayed if it wasn't for my then ex. However, while I lived in the old shop with him at Trewellard, I had a pure paranormal experience that I have no explanation for, but it showed me that not every experience is bad. Not every experience is terrifying, and it just felt Natural. I didn't freak out.

I was sat in bed watching the television. The latch on the door next to me went up and the door creaked open ever so slightly. I looked towards the door and all I saw was a grey circular blob just float in through the door and disappear into the wall. It felt like something was just saying hello. I felt nothing bad towards it or from it, and just carried on watching the television. I just accepted it. I loved that little house and living that close to the cliffs. Botallack and Levant Beam Engine were my dream places to visit. It was so nice to go to the cliff tops in the sunshine and then watching the wintery storms rolling in. The huge waves that would crash in over the ancient rocks below. I could taste the salty spray in the air. Magic. However, it was partially me who screwed things up. I was still so damaged and still trying to fill the void in my life any way I could, that I didn't take his feelings into consideration. I wasn't a good partner. I did try, but I just wasn't fully there. Things broke down, as they inevitably would. He had some mental health problems anyway and would often say to me that he was going to annoy me until I left the house. I would then say that I would go and sleep in the car. He would then beg me to stay. Then would start telling me to go again. It was one long, vicious, tiring circle. After the last few years of doing pretty much what I wanted, it was hard to realise just how controlled I had been. I did not function well under control. I had left home and was living with another version of my father. It wasn't a place I wanted to be, and I was fearful of what he would do if I left. I just had to get out.

I had to leave and move back home. The night I left, he pinned me to the wall by my face and hissed at me, "Kiss me one more time". It's safe to say I did not hang around. Going back home wasn't ideal. It was something that I didn't want to do, but I had no choice. I had nowhere else to go. I still wasn't talking to the rest of my family. It was like the only place and person I had was Trevor. I was very aware that it was very much my choice, but I also felt that with my emotional problems that I still wasn't ready to go it alone. I needed some sort of crutch.

I had a steady job and time passed fine. I cohabited with Trevor, who was slowly aging, and I could see he wasn't what he used to be. He was still incredibly selfish and arrogant and everything else, but he was slower. I was taller, stronger, bigger. I worked, spent my money and just got on with life. Hannah had gone back off to university, so I hung out with Joanna and we did our thing. I was always so thankful for my friends. We weren't just ever friends. We were and are all one big family. Other people came and went. There was another relationship around 2009, he was so nice, but a serial cheat. I know for some reason I had to meet him. He was persistent with the idea that I was cheating on him, so one day I set up a fake profile online out of curiosity, to see if I could find him online. Online dating was the main way of meeting people. He messaged me straight away with photos of the nude nature, so I knew what his game was. I arranged to meet him at a time when he thought that the real me would be at work. When I showed up on the doorstep, he was taken aback. I left immediately. I only bring up those past relationships as links to experiences I have had. Those episodes of my life are mainly private, but I like some context as I move through time. While online dating just after this, I was chatting to someone from a few miles down the road so decided to meet. This is where I can only describe it as I had my first medium experience. If I had not met the last guy, then I'd not have met this fellow and what happened would never have happened. I arrived at this person's place and texted to say I couldn't really find it. They came to meet me and said that no-one could ever find it. When I went inside, I felt something. It felt like a heaviness, a melancholy. We went into the lounge. I can't remember what we were talking about, but it transpired that he had been sleeping with my ex the whole time we were together. My ex was a total rat bag. I didn't have much faith in relationships, but I was still trying. By some odd coincidence, I had gone and met that guy he was cheating on me with. That was very strange. I looked around the lounge and stated how cold it was. I felt the hairs on the back of my neck going up. I felt like I had been there before. Seriously strong déjà vu. The man then said, "There's a story to this place.".

As he said that, it was like the knowledge had been given to me again. Only this time, I knew. I just knew it was bang on. I had been looking at this little, black dog CD holder that was pointing towards the television. I said very clearly and confidently that someone had died of a drug overdose in that corner. I pointed to where his television was and led him through my explanation. It wasn't as if I was explaining myself, I was just stating the facts of what I felt with the information that I had been presented with. I said that that was the focal point of it in the corner. The corner was where the man died and that is where he had remained since. I didn't see a spirit in front of me. I saw it in my mind's eye, and I felt it. Empaths can feel everything and that is what happened to me. I felt the surge of the heroin in the needle and the feeling of relaxation as the high kicked in. I then felt the panic and confusion as I, well he, started to drift away. We were totally powerless to pull ourselves back. I felt every second of it. He was unable to get back. It was a mere fraction of a second, but I felt it. I explained how he had been led by the spirit of the man to put his television there, so that he would focus on the spot. It felt like the spirit was upset as he hadn't been noticed in all that time. Everything linked in my mind. I had seen the black dog CD holder again and, in my mind, I saw Snoop. When I thought of Snoop, I immediately thought of what I had said to my friend about my visitor being him, then he disappeared. Moved on. I linked that to this man. My black dog was pointing at him. The dog had wanted acknowledgement so that he could move on. The man who had died of the overdose wanted the same. Snoop was showing me. I told the owner of the place that the man just wanted acknowledgement. He wanted someone to see him, feel him and understand. He didn't want to die. It just happened. He was unwell and had an addiction. I felt that urge to live in the panic as he drifted away from himself. I felt that to my core. As soon as I said all of this, I felt, and I am very sure he felt the room change too, it lifted. The atmosphere was lighter. I felt that chill I get up my spine when something is right, that the spirit of the person who had overdosed had moved on. I understood everything in that moment. Every essence of my being felt wired just for a few seconds, then it faded away. I felt drained and elated at the same time. That was empathic, as I could feel exactly how he had felt.

As soon as the room changed and lifted, we both sat there in shock for a good few minutes. It was like an energy field in the room. I felt light, but also heavy, just sat there. I was slightly floating out of my body, but tethered so I didn't stray far. I thought that maybe I had caused that. The spirit and I had somehow manipulated the energy of the environment to enable him to move on. The person I had gone to meet was extremely shocked and slightly disbelieving at what we had both just witnessed. He wanted sex. I said no. I realised I wasn't there for that. I did believe in fate and wondered if I was meant to be there in that moment, for that purpose. Not for the guy I met, but for the person trapped there. I then made my excuses and left. As I left, I felt that I had been drawn there for the task of moving that spirit on. I felt that was right and that was the thing to do. I felt that in my heart and mind. I didn't try to do anything. I put the bits of knowledge together and it happened. I was learning to listen to these little hints and follow little signs. Just certain chills that would tell me when I was on the right path. Intuition. Relationship debris was piling up on my highway, but it didn't matter, I was still looking. Still hopeful. Ever searching for the one.

In 2010, I saw one of my favourite bands, the Doves, at the Eden Project at home in Cornwall. The Eden Project is an old china clay quarry that was recycled and turned into massive biomes, which have all sorts of wonderful plants and forestry. They have created such beautiful ground and points of interest, that thousands of people flock there. The live music shows are always done on a grassy patch at the front of the giant biomes. As the sun goes down, the domes all light up different colours. Music was always life changing for me. Ever since I had been seeing live music, it added an extra magic to all songs for me. I really connected with the artists. Albums seemed to come to me at a time when I needed them the most. It was like music healed me. Feeder, The Twilight Sad, White Lies, We were Promised Jetpacks and the Engineers shaped my daily life. These bands guided me and soothed me. Elated me, motivated me and entertained me.

It was also in 2010 that I began to reconcile with some of my family. I worked a lot so rarely saw Trevor, but my sister got in touch with me and told me that my grandad was ill. He was dying. I didn't know how long he had left, but I rushed over to see him. I remember driving over and feeling hesitant, as I sat outside in the car looking at the bungalow. It was the right thing to do and it was my family. The people who I had been closest to, I was now so distanced from. It had been so long and it was a bit of a shock, but we both had a cry, and everything was all right. At least I hoped it was all right, because I really loved my grandad and to see him aged and unwell, wasn't a sight that appealed to me. Even when I left from the visit, I had anxiety that they thought it would be an empty romantic gesture of me just showing up towards the end. In my mind, I wanted to make everything all right and I didn't want my grandad and family to be in pain. Things are just how they are. They were the way they were. I wasn't there when he passed, which I couldn't have done at that stage as I would have had to have seen and spoken to my mum, which I wasn't strong enough to do. The more time we spent apart, the harder thoughts were of reconciling fully. I was halfway there. I remember sitting with my nan and she knew he was close, she just wanted him to go, for his own sake. I thought that I would always remember him that way, how he was near the end, but I didn't.

I always remembered him in a beautiful way. Always working, saying all the things that amused me as a child, telling me off over the cuckoo clock and playing with my Mighty Maxes with me. She kept him at home as long as she could, and I will always love and respect her for that. She was stronger than all of us. I felt like a horrible, selfish child for having had my head buried in the sand for so long. I had been out just getting wasted and living my days away. I did give all my family a lot of thought, but I guess I was just so damaged that it was taking me a very long time to process everything. I was on a constant journey and I felt like I had to do it alone. Like I was alone. I could always rely on me. My grandad's dying wish was that I spoke to my mum again, which at that stage I just couldn't do. Joanna accompanied me to the crematorium and she rocked side to side, enjoying the music on her day out. That made me smile before I had a mental breakdown and had to flee to the car after the service. I just wasn't mentally strong enough to deal with everyone. I stayed and held it together as long as I physically could. There have been few occasions my friends have seen me crack and that was certainly one of them.

I continued seeing my nan from then on. She understood my anger and pain and had told me all sorts of stories about my dad and the things he did. She told me about the things they had done to try and help me as well. I understood a bit more. My nan knew how violent my dad was and didn't want to get too involved, as my dad would threaten them both all the time. They must have seen how broken my mother was when she returned home to them after that fateful night when she finally fled Trevor. I began to empathise with my mother. I realised that when I was younger and mum would drop us home, that I'd feel ill every time. I instinctively felt that it was part me and I was also picking up on how my mother felt dropping us back to that evil man. Even at that young age, I was reading how she felt. I knew she was on antidepressants her whole life, partly because of the things he did to her. I knew how she felt, because I had been through things as well. It just wasn't spoken about in our family. My nan learnt a lot of the extent of how he treated me and Laura, and she was truly sorry. I was truly sorry for not seeing my nan and grandad for so long. In the end though, we healed our rifts, that I don't think really ever existed, we were always tighter in heart or mind. I only blamed one person for it all and that was Trevor. If he had never done any of the things he had done to us, then we would have been a whole family. Instead we were all broken and jagged in our own ways. So much anguish caused by one man who destroyed everything and everyone he met. We had all been affected by Trevor and Alison in our own way. I was angrier that all of us lived in misery, when one of us could have spoken up. I guess that's the thing about being abused. You don't always speak up until it's too late. I did finally understand why my mother fled and left my dad, but I still didn't know how she could have left her children with him. I understood that he broke her down and scared her. I really understood, which was scary because I didn't know now how I would react in that situation. I'd imagine I'd stab fucking Trevor before letting him take my children, but we all act and respond to things differently. She did what she had to do and what she thought was best. I knew that. I felt that. I was healing slowly and surely.

I felt like I was growing stronger in mind and decided it was time to get away from Trevor. I had to move out. One day I just was standing there in the flat, looking out of the window at that familiar view of Carn Brea. His television was on in his lounge, blaring as usual. It was so loud. At that stage, everything he said made me cringe, every request. Every task. I was sick to the back teeth of him. I felt like I had given him the best years of my life and for what? I just had to get the money and get out. I needed to find a deposit for a place. Hannah and Joanna helped me with this. I spoke to my nan about it, but she was cagey about being a guarantor on it. I guess as I hadn't been around much, it was a bit dodgy in case I missed my rent and I didn't want my nan to worry about me.

I occasionally thought about the shadow person I had seen so many years ago and had experienced a lot since then. I would feel my grandad around me. I don't care what anyone says, but I did. I had heard things. I had seen things, so I believed fully in something. However, I still blocked it as I worried about seeing that figure. Face to face. The full apparition. I didn't want to see that. I imagined I'd be terrified and wet myself with fear. It was strange as sometimes I would fully submerge myself in what I thought I could do. Then suddenly it would be like I'd caught myself and had to shut it all out again, before I over thought it and passed myself off as crazy. Once I finally made it out of the home where Trevor lived, I was free. I was truly physically free of Trevor and that flat. I was living on my own. My own space, my bills. Everything mine. True freedom.

Plain-an-Gwarry, 2011 – The Sanctuary

I moved into the church in Plain-an-Gwarry, that I had played inside of years before. I remembered all those years ago when I said to my friends, "I'm going to live there one day!" as I pointed up to the window on the left. The huge stained-glass windows were broken and damaged, but they had been renovated and rejuvenated. Inside the beautiful stained-glass windows stretched from floor to ceiling on two walls of the bedroom and the lounge. The mezzanine inside was so beautiful. I felt so at peace here. My own space. Own home. Own life. Everything was wonderful, no interruptions. No mess from other people. No constant reminders. I loved how the sunlight came through the stained glass and cast the colours red, blue and green onto the floors and walls. This was truly a beautiful place to be. I felt connected to something. I was overjoyed that it was the very same church that I had played in as a child when I lived down the road in The Old Dairy. Back then it was just an old Wesleyan chapel that had fallen into ruin and disrepair. We used to throw stones at the windows. I'd never have done that as an adult. I wanted to stay there and preserve it. I had a lot of anxiety over the years.

I self-managed. I had never actually sought help to see if I was depressed. It was obvious, and I did what I could to get by. Living on my own was a fresh start, but it also increased my anxieties as everything was down to me.

I hadn't had any nightmares for a long time. This night was different. It was probably due to the anxieties I'd had recently regarding moving and getting everything sorted. I was walking up the road towards the house in Agar Road. As I walked home from work in the dark, I heard a sudden screech of tyres. It must have been near midnight and it was a quiet town, so it was inevitable that anyone would hear a sound out of the blue. There was a gold Vauxhall Carlton speeding down the road, seemingly out of control. I couldn't see inside as the windows were blacked out. It was going so fast that I barely had time to jump out of the way as it hit a lamppost and went skidding sideways into a wall on the road where I was. The wall was made of sturdy granite and there was a mass of tangled metal and smoke now rising. I heard the hissing of the engine. My heart was racing as I just sat there on the floor, shocked at how quickly that had just happened. Thankful for a second that I was still alive, and then suddenly running towards the car to see if there was anyone injured in there. The street remained silent. There was no-one looking out of the windows or anything. Time seemed to have stood still. Like the shock had caused a fracture in time and I was just frozen in the moment. I turned to look to my left and realised I was outside the house in Agar Road. The car had hit its wall. As I approached the car, the door was flung open. I knew straight away that the person inside was not injured. The door swung open far too easily. As I stood frozen to the spot for a second, a very tall man stepped out of the car. His face was covered. He must have been six foot four inches tall. I couldn't see any facial features. Just a black covering. He must have been able to see me. I recall semi sniggering to myself and thinking, "that's probably why he crashed, dick.". Then I came to and into the moment. I looked at his hand. He had a shotgun in his hand. It looked a lot like the shotgun I had recalled my father owning when I was a child. I remembered playing with the bullets as a kid. Trevor being the ever vigilant and present parent. Instinctively I prepared to step backwards. I was still in shock from the car speeding towards me, so everything seemed to be happening in slow motion. Even though I was in my mid-twenties, I could still run. So, I did. The man came after me. I sprinted down this road, tripped and rolled over.

As I rolled over, I looked up and saw the car crashed into the wall just in front of me. What? The guy was getting out of the car again. I turned to run the other way and again fell. Something forced me down. Again, when I looked up, the car was in front of me. How could everything move? I did question if the car had hit me and I was dead, and this was my spirit jumping around in some sort of purgatory. I knew where I was meant to go. I had been led here. I turned and looked up behind me at the house in Agar Road. I knew I had to go inside. I looked around again as the man got out of the car. I turned my head away and there he was again on the other side of me, getting out of that car. My gut told me to go into the house. My head told me also. I didn't want to. I could already feel what was in there.

It felt like fingers creeping over my face. Tendrils growing into my ears and nose. Hesitantly I edged away from the man getting out of the car again and towards the front of the house. The windows were like eyes staring down on me. I got to the front door, which was slightly ajar. It creaked open as I pushed on the heavy wood. I stepped inside the house and the door slowly squealed shut. I went straight into the lounge on the right. The fish tank my dad used to have was there, but was glowing red like blood casting an eerie light over the room. I ran back out into the hallway. I looked up at the stairs. I did not want to go up there. The banister invited me to touch it and trace it as it went up and around. I could visualise the whole upstairs anyway. I did not want to see what was at the end. I ran down the hallway past the shadow man's bedroom and into the back room. I could see straight out of the kitchen window. It was exactly as it was when I had lived there. I thought to myself that I should empty the cupboards, because all the food would have gone off. We had moved out years before, so there would be rats and all sorts. I ran out the back of the house as I heard the front door slam. The tall, dark man was in the house. I went into the shed and looked for a weapon of some sort. I saw the pictures that I had seen all those years before. I remembered the man. That story. I remembered the shadow figure I had seen in that very house, behind me. I wasn't sure if the man had moved on or if he had remained. I could hear items crashing inside the house as if someone was flipping furniture, looking for me. I came out of the shed and as I did, I looked up past the porch and to the back window that led into the shadow man room. The tall guy was in there and just happened to turn his head in my direction and look out. I couldn't see his face but I am sure our eyes met for a second.

I ran so hard up the side of the house and through the side gate. I was gone, a speck in the distance. I ran towards my church. I had to run along the main road, but I thought I would be seen so I took little back lanes I had known as a child. I ran down the road past the tyre shop on the right. Past the garage on the left and Erica, my first home. I continued to run and then decided to turn left down the side of the houses and into the valley. I thought if I ran a long way, then I may not be followed. I didn't know or was even able to think if this person or thing chasing me knew the area. My home was aptly named The Sanctuary. That's where I was headed. It was a good couple of miles away, but I ran like I had never run before. Down through the childhood valley I'd played in and ridden my bike through. I came back up by the old people's home and looped back through West Park, where I had once laid my head. For now, the church would be my safe place. For this is what it had been to me. A refuge. A place to be happy. My only regret was that my nan hadn't made it to see the flat before she had passed away, but I was convinced that like others, she had visited me. One night I came home and heard the creaking of someone walking across the floor upstairs. For some reason I didn't want to investigate the window that covered both floors, so chose to potter around downstairs until whatever was up there had dissipated. Later that night I was very tired, but got out of bed to go to the toilet and as I walked down the stairs and round the small corner, it was like I bumped into someone that was not there and turned around and walked promptly straight back to bed. I wasn't scared by this though. I always thought that it may have been nan visiting finally. It was comforting.

There was no comfort now in this situation. The streetlamps were all out. Everywhere was dark. Desolate. I was blindly running. I didn't really know if the man was giving chase, but something inside was yelling so loudly, booming at me to RUN, RUN, RUN. I was suddenly running out of Redruth. I had already run all the way past Plain-an-Gwarry, down past the old brewery, along the bottom of the main town, which was very small. I had run under the viaduct, gone right up at Trewirgie Hill, left past my old infant school, up past the cricket field and onto the road to Four Lanes. I was moving so fast. I didn't care at this stage if the man was behind me. I was running for my life. Suddenly something struck me hard and painfully. I felt something pierce my skin. Was it a gunshot? I didn't know. I felt pain and warm wetness. Suddenly I saw the man. Whatever was covering his face had slipped a little. In a daze, I thought how hot he must be under that. It was almost pitch black, so I couldn't see his face. I just got up again and bolted. My heart was bursting through my chest at that point. My lungs felt like lead and were heaving. But I continued. I ran along the roads, through the fields. Dodging any car lights that came and headed out towards the lake. Stithians Dam was the place I decided to head to. It was an open place that I could see all around.

As I ran, I questioned myself as to why this could be happening. I hadn't done anything to anyone. I was very non-offensive. I lived a quiet life and didn't really see that many people. I could sometimes speak my mind which would annoy people, but that isn't really a cause to chase someone down with an old shot gun. Suddenly a car came out at me again from a turning. There was no way that this guy could know where I was. I continued to flee. I ran faster and harder. My lungs burnt for more oxygen. My legs felt heavy and hot. My eyes streamed. I headed around the side of the lake as it went off road. The car could not follow here. The ground was flat, so I kind of thought that the car could go through it if the driver was crazy enough and drove fast enough. My anxiety level was critical. The car could have been anywhere. He could have been on foot. My thoughts were just racing. I was just running. Getting away. I found a cluster of trees and hid behind it for a few minutes, gathering my breath. Everywhere was black now as the glow of any windows on houses or any random streetlamps, in the distance, had gone. The clouds unexpectedly cleared though and there was a quarter moon glowing poorly in the sky. This cast shadows where I was, but I could see all around and I knew that 85% of the area was water. It was a flooded reservoir that had been built many years before. Dark, deep and cool. It could also be loud and fierce when it was overflowing. It had two sides to it. The Yin and the Yang. All the paths that I would take then at that moment would lead me to one place, and that would be the place for the show down. That would be the place where I either became the man I had wanted to be, or I didn't. There was no other choice. No other way. It was time to confront everything that had been chasing me down. Everything that had frightened me or scared me over the years. Every part of every experience had empowered me for this moment. Although I had been broken and had been weak, that was in the past. I was stronger. Stronger than I had ever known.

Chapter 8

The Damned

I'm close to the edge,
I want to fall all the way down,
You're making me, close to the edge,
I'm gonna fall, when I touch the ground

I jumped over the gate and onto the dam. There was a small building in the middle that was always unlocked, so I ran there. There was no-one inside. I could hear the whooshing of the overspill hitting the solid floor down below. I was shivering with the cold, but at the same time sweating because of the exertion. I could hear the screeching of tyres again. It sounded like a car was driving fast and then reversing quickly and then accelerating again. It was searching for me. Repeating this as if looking in every area for me. There was an old glass bottle on the floor next to me. I promptly smashed the bottom off it, so that I could use it if I had to. Not as effective as a gun, but if needs be, it would work. I didn't dwell too much on his thought as I had never really considered killing anybody, but when it comes to self-preservation, do we really know what anyone is capable of? If you had to fight for your own survival, what would you be prepared to do?

I knew that people I loved had died and I wondered, just for a second, if it would be so hard to join them. Something in that moment in me, gave up. It was purely for a second, but I then got up and carried on. I had to keep going. Keep on moving. Keep on fighting. This was my life. I felt inside that I had worked so hard to stay alive to this stage and age. I wanted more life, more time. It wasn't so much the thought of dying. It was the manner in which it would happen. I always imagined it would be painful and drawn out. I did not imagine for one moment that getting shot would be quick and pain free.

The car noises in the distance had gone quiet. I didn't really know how long it had been since they had stopped as I had been shivering and staring out of the window into the deep, despairing water, self-chatting internally and over thinking at a million miles an hour. I had lost all sense of time. I could hear the cool wind blowing outside of the building and the lapping of the water as it hit the back of the building. The dam was about one hundred and fifty feet high and below, the shallow water lay littered with large rocks that local people had obviously thrown over to see what sort of impact they made. Suddenly realising what a bad idea it was to be found cowering in a building with no route for escape, I was precipitously out of the door and running the opposite way. The dam was very long anyway, so I could get a good bit of distance between me and this mad man.

"BANG!" A shot went off somewhere behind me. I ducked without hesitation, not knowing if anything could hit me or if the distance was too great. Either way, it let me know that the person was in pursuit and he knew where I was. I thought to myself through all the random panicked thoughts, that this guy must be fast. Very fast indeed.

As I ran faster and faster, jumping over the branches that hung out of hedges from around the edge of the reservoir, I suddenly tripped. There was a huge root sticking out of the ground that I would have normally spotted, but due to the speed I was running, I caught my foot directly in it and cracked my ankle. It made a horrible squelchy pop. I winced out in pain as quietly as I could, but when I tried to get up and run on my leg, I collapsed and the pain made me pass out. I must have woken a few seconds later, but I heard twigs snapping and breaking. The splosh of a puddle. This man was not far behind me. I could feel the excruciating pain in my ankle, but I dragged myself on. Trying to move out of sight and go a bit near the water's edge, so that the lapping sounds would hide my presence.

"BANG!" again. Something struck me. It felt like it was a tennis ball or something. Or like someone had poked me hard. I felt a warmth wash over me. I looked down, dazed and confused, and saw the blood oozing from my side. A bullet had hit me. It had skimmed, but hit me hard enough on the way past to take a chunk of flesh out and turn my clothes dark red with the fresh blood. I suddenly hit the floor, harder than when I had tripped over the root. Arms out flat and cheek to the ground.

I was transported a million miles away. I pulled myself up off of the floor, but it was a polished marble floor. There was no mud or darkness. No snapping of twigs and twitches of anxiety. There was music playing in the background. It sounded very, very old. I didn't recognise it, so knew that it was nothing I owned. It was truly old, maybe even Victorian. The room didn't seem to have many features, there was just a lot of light. Blinding white light. I pondered how strange this was as I looked down at the marble floor again. It appeared to move momentarily beneath my feet, dropping down and reappearing back up in a fraction of a second. I saw a re-enactment of something. It looked like me in my old house on Agar Road. I was looking down upon myself in my bed. I saw myself wake up. Terrified. I wanted to reach out and comfort myself, but there was nothing I could do. I could see the look of absolute horror on my own face. I could only silently look at myself. That was the night the shadow figure had visited. I saw time move and change. There I was again, fast asleep, laying on the floor of the lounge. I watched myself wake up and look terrified again. I yelled to try and console myself, but I heard no sound. No voice. I couldn't see what I looked like, my physical presence, but I could see my own face screaming back at me. Suddenly time was slipping away again and I was stood outside of Glyngarth in Lanner, in the rain. There was a flash of lightning as I stood underneath the streetlamp. I was looking up at my bedroom window. Watching myself. Watching me. How had this come to be?

"There's still time", came a subtle whisper from somewhere in my mind. There was nothing I could do to emphasise where this man with a gun had come from, but why was I suddenly having this bizarre dream. Then it clicked in my mind. The turning of the mind, when you suddenly know what everything means. I was in a dream in a dream. What was it trying to tell me? What did the shadow person want from me? Was the shadow person who I thought it was? The entities. The demons. The spirits. Why did it call to me? Did it want me back, did it want to hurt me?

I was suddenly back on the ground near the reservoir. I didn't know if I had opened my eyes or not. I felt weightless, as if I was still attached to my body, but my body wasn't really attached to anything anymore. Like I was contacting the ground, but I couldn't feel the ground. Yet I knew its firmness was still there, touching me. The dull aching slowly crept in as I tried to open my eyes. They flicked open and all I could see was confusing mist around me. My fear suddenly subsided and I wasn't afraid. Everything seemed calm. Quiet. Dark and tranquil. My head throbbed, my ankle ached. My side felt stingy. There was definite pain now. As I came to my senses a bit more, the floor spun. My stomach dropped. The pain was much worse. "So, sleeping beauty awakes", a voice jeered at me. "Who... what?" I croaked, my mouth sore and dry. As I came to my senses a little more, I realised I was back in the centre of the dam. I was right above the basin at the highest point. If I was to go over the railings, then that would be it. The end. This man had dragged me, possibly carried me back to this spot and thrown me against a railing. He had clearly sat there waiting for me to wake up, so that he could see whatever it was he wanted. Maybe he wanted to see my eyes full of fear.

My eyes, they were so full of grit and mud or whatever was fogging up my mind. I couldn't really make out the man's face. I wasn't tied, but I felt like I couldn't move. I was in such pain that all I could do was lay there, half crippled with wounds and burning eyes. "All you had to do was help", a chilling voice croaked. Sinister, but slightly familiar.

"What?" I uttered, I could barely breathe. I tried to take in deep lungful's of air, but couldn't. I didn't really know what to say.

"I last forever. In the darkness, where I was born. Put on this earth for this life, this time around. There is a reason and a purpose and a fate. They all exist at the same time. Everything exists at the same time.".

I did not understand what was going on. I really had no clue. I was a captive audience to what sounded like a monologue.

"How could you remember, you never knew. I have been there all your life. Seeing moments, waiting... waiting for the moments to...", he paused. "To see if you could see what no one else saw.". This was very confusing to me, but I could not move. I could only listen. My mind swirled. Everything was spinning anyway now. My heart was bursting behind my ribs. I was totally spent. I had nothing more to give.

"I have dwelled in the dark places, the shadows, watching. Waiting. I have been with you.". I began to think this was the rantings of a madman. "You were closest to figuring it out, every day.". "That house.". "But what does this have to do with me?", I questioned as I gripped my side and tried to roll. I felt a foot or something heavy push me and roll me back into place.

"You saw them", he replied.

"I watched you..." he paused, "nearby". The figure walked away from me and looked over into the water.

I couldn't really see him, I just knew he had gone out of my eyeline. "What... who are you?" I asked, my voice low. My mind felt dizzy. My stomach was churning and all the pain made me curl up further into a ball. I wondered why I wasn't already dead.

I could hear the anger in the man's voice. He almost hissed out the things he said. Nasty, negative thoughts. All sorts of things I had thought about myself over the years. The anguish. The pain. The horror. That fear. How dare someone else tell me how I feel. Tell me what I am, when they know nothing. I felt the anger growing inside of me. I felt a burning. It wasn't pain. I was really pissed off. I was angry. Furious from everything I had been through in that evening. Everything I had ever been put through by anyone, including Trevor and Alison.

"What's your name?", I questioned again. My mind was so fuzzy, so foggy. I saw the silhouette stood over me. "Just do what you have to do", I surrendered. Broken. Nothing left. Silence.

"I've had enough of this shit, you come to me for something. You won't say. Do what you have to do, fucker". Still nothing. I felt myself lifting in the air. I was suddenly getting up on my own feet. I felt a warmth all over my body and felt healing from the inside. I was feeling stronger than I ever had before. I came to again. It wasn't me getting to my legs. I was being lifted into the air by this massive and strong man and the warmth was the blood spilling from my wound. I recall looking down at a small puddle of it on the floor and seeing the moonlight reflected in it. My eyes were clearing. I could see.

"Just throw me over", I snapped. That surge I had felt wasn't real. It must have been my body's last ebb of fight, trying to get me to snap out of it.

Something inside of me clicked. As I felt this person, dark shape lift me up, I grabbed hold of him and somehow over balanced him, for his footing suddenly changed below me. I pulled myself against him using his weight and brought my knee to his face. I felt it impact against him. I had to try. Everything was silent as we both fought in the pale moonlight. I was really on my feet now. Standing. So cold, that the pain had all but gone away. I still couldn't fully see, but I knew the width of the dam and made good use of the space. I could feel that everything had been building to this moment. The confrontation. The final confrontation. I had taken a lot over the years and I was going to fight for my life. I had been battling my whole life. I had been fighting for a long time and had been in fear for even longer. There was no room for anymore fear. It was my life and I needed to take back control. He beat me down well. Reigned blow after blow after blow. I fell to my knees, face bloodied and swelling. I longed to escape, but that was it, I had nothing left. I didn't understand. I had survived so much. Was this the end?

"All you feel is pain", he screamed at me as he kicked me in the stomach, sending me backwards hard against the railing of the dam. I should have known I was going over there. Why did I bring myself here for this ending?
"You see everything, but ignore…. Everything.".
"You feel everything… but, nothing.".
"Thwack!" As he punched me again. It felt as if he was

213

just swinging his arms around and they were battering me with ease. I could feel my body crumple. Soul ebbing away. After everything I had been through, this was it. This was the end. No music or sunset soul food was going to get me out of this. I remember thinking, where are all your crystals now? I found a sudden and unexpected energy. Light filled me and I sprang to my feet. To my rescue. This was how it ended. I was filled with a knowing, an assurance. I looked up as I rose and grabbed out at the man still dark, the moonlight had faded behind the dark clouds and rain gently began to fall. It was like slow motion. Dawning realisation. I felt a confidence that everything was going to be all right. I was fine. I don't know how I knew, it was just there. Just information given to me freely like air. As I grabbed out, I took hold of the rail and swung with all my weight at the figure. He didn't seem as large as he did before. Maybe I was just out of my mind with fear and dread, dreadful tiredness and exhaustion. He was smaller. I swung with all my weight and felt him go over the rail and clunk against the other side, as he grabbed out for me and the railings. I saw the moon come out from the cloud behind me. It was reflecting on the rail. I felt its tiny glow on my back. And it began to light up the whole dam, spreading across it like fire. I looked down at the hand that had grabbed hold of me and felt myself going over the railing as well. As I looked down, I made eye contact with the man. We looked directly into each other and then it all made sense. As our eyes met and locked almost four inches apart, I recalled everything. I felt everything. I was looking at me. The person staring back at me was me. I had been chasing myself, grappling and killing myself, searching for myself. I was fighting with myself. Somehow over all these years, I had been watching over myself. Waiting for myself to catch up, sending myself messages. Watching. Waiting. A divine fate sending me messages years apart. Everything happened at the same time, past, present and future. It was the darker side of me, the person I could have become. A twisted inhumane version of me who hadn't got better. He had got bitter, but he still looked out for me, over the years and through time. Always there. I had never been alone. In that moment of realisation, I felt an odd comfort that I had always been there for me. Always. Maybe it was some twisted memory of me looking back, but I knew I was never alone. I just didn't understand it. Now I did. I had seen me countless times. When I felt the energies and saw the shadow man, I was always there on another plain watching myself from another time. I had ignored everything for so long, that the only way to make me see, was to try and kill me to make me realise what I had and how far I had come. I created this myself. Like a poltergeist. The bad side to my good. Both needing each other.

I felt so calm in the glistening of the moonlight. As I pulled at myself, I began to kick out. I was trying to get free and get back over the railing. The other me was only holding on with one hand and another hand on me. Pulling at me, silently clawing trying to tear me down. I kicked out contacting with his, my face. I heard a "Humph" sound.

All this time I had been in pain, I was fighting against myself. I was fighting to be heard. Even to be seen. I just had to recognise myself. My darkness was something that I needed to face and then everything would be all right. I realised that everything I felt and had endured was just and that it was part of the journey. I had to learn to trust myself again. I hadn't for a long time. That was the moment. The thought fell into place. I knew no matter what anyone, living or dead did to me, it would never be as hard or horrible as I was on myself. We are all our own worst critics. I looked down at myself as I let go of the rail with a smile. Shock covered the face of the other me. I looked up as the rail sped by and then we began to plummet. I looked up at the bright moonlight, smiling. Taking a deep breath before we struck the basin far below.

I woke up in my own bed at home. I knew halfway through that that was a dream, but I realised I couldn't wake myself up and was just going with it. I believed I was lucid dreaming as I spent so long trying to take control and run away. I felt some sort of internal healing as I had investigated myself. I had taken on the worst enemy I'd ever have, myself. And I won. I remembered that smile as I fell. Pure knowing, contentment and peace. I didn't need someone else to save me. I didn't need someone else to come along and complete me. I had always been complete. I had saved myself.

Chapter 9

The Final Nightmare

Karma, karma,
The end of all the drama
For all the hurt, you're gonna burn
My, my, my Delilah

<u>2013 to 2019</u>

I had long since left home and Trevor continued to age. I took no pleasure in it, but he was weaker. Reliant. That wasn't my life. It caused me a great deal of stress to continue to go over there and do tasks for him. As a grown man, I was able to make my own choices, own decisions, and Trevor was just a burden. It wasn't like I had had a glowing childhood and he deserved to be looked after and pampered. No. I stayed out of some twisted sense of duty and to show that I wasn't the same as him. I was a better person. He knew that deep down. All my wounds were healing. I was getting older. I felt a little wiser. As did the people I knew. I watched them grow and change and move on with their lives. Most settling down and having children. It had taken many, many years, but I finally saw that karma would prevail. The one person who Trevor had abused the most, was the only person that he had left. The only person he had in the world for him, was the one he had done the least for. What did he think that I would do? Was he so arrogant to think that I would have stayed until the bitter end to serve him? I imagined he would tell me I should be grateful from dragging me up. I had stayed around and even I couldn't take it for much longer. I used to go around two or three times a week and clean or cook. I hated doing it, but I did it. I still think it was some sort of fear or power he had over me. I got on with my own life, living in Illogan. Walking down the fields. Just enjoying my life. My peace. My time.

One day in 2016, I just had enough. I had reached the point where I couldn't do it anymore. I couldn't pretend that he had done nothing to me, my family. I disowned Trevor, for all the things he had done to me as a child, for everything he had done to my sister and the rest of my family. The day I walked out of that flat and left there, I knew it would be the last time I saw him. I knew I was free. People say grow up, take responsibility for your own actions, but Trevor was to blame for the way myself and Laura were brought up. We would have been a lot more rounded and well-developed people if he hadn't had an influence over our lives. He was a brutal, bitter man and I did not want to turn out the same. I hadn't. I didn't know the cause of my change and mind being made up, but it happened. I had just had enough of the bullshit, the pretending. I came to the conclusion that he did not look after me as a child, so why should I have to look after him in his old age? I should have had a wonderful, caring father who would have been loved and respected. Not all families are so lucky. I knew Trevor was now a sad, old man and there was no chance that he would come after me or stop me. He had no fight left in him. I repeated it many times, but he got what he deserved. It took a lot of courage for me to finally leave him behind, but everything I had been through had made me strong. And now I was strong enough to stand up and be the man I had always wanted to be.

I wrote Trevor a letter, laying out everything that I remembered him doing to me as a child. I told him all about what Alison had done to me. I put every detail that had happened, including things about Alison that even my own father had never known. Every injustice, every dark secret in that letter. I didn't hold back. He was an adult, so he should have remembered a lot more than me. I knew that as he read the letter, he would know I was telling the truth. He would know what he had done to me. How he had darkened and twisted his two children's childhoods. It was something that I should have done a very, very long time before then. I posted the letter. I received some messages on Facebook telling me that I needed to contact my father, as he was in hospital. I frankly didn't care. People called me all sorts, as they thought I should have been a dutiful son and been there for him. Why? He did nothing for me as a child, other than emotionally and physically abuse me. I had no allegiance to the man. No respect. I had always been a firm believer that respect is earnt, not expected.

I explained the situation to his friend Rodney and said if he wanted a copy of the letter, he was welcome to take it to the hospital. I sent it in an envelope to Rodney knowing he would read it, which probably didn't sit well with my dad, but I was glad someone else would bear witness to it. Rodney apologised for everything that he had also let happen to me as a child. Rodney had always hated Alison; Laura would later tell me this.

Then just after that, Trevor passed away. I never even asked what he died off. It was information that was of no use to me. There was a huge sense of relief. I thought that I would break at that point. I thought that when it came to news of the funeral, that I would feel awful for abandoning him. That there would be an outpouring of emotion, but when it came to that moment, I felt nothing. I held onto my freedom. I then began to feel bad because I felt nothing. I came to the realisation that that was what he had done to me. To us. To my family. I was finally free. I felt free. Whatever grip Trevor had had over me my whole life, it was now gone. There was no love, no pain, no upset, not even any hate. I was truly free. My father was dead and he could no longer hurt me. I had told him all the injustices he had done to me and that was that. I recalled how I felt when my grandad, nan and uncle had passed away. How painful that was. How distressing it was. I felt none of that. That was Trevor's karma. To be left alone. To die alone. That was karma. I never ever truly believed in it, but there it was working right in front of me. My mum told me that she had told him years before that he would end up dying alone. I thought it spoke volumes that not one family member was going to be at his funeral.

After thirty years, I was strong enough to stand up to the man who had beaten me down, taken every ounce of confidence I'd ever had, destroyed me. I never received a response to the letter and soon heard from Trevor's friends that as next of kin, I would have to pay for the funeral. That didn't sound right. He had life insurance and a will after all. I said I would have to sign him over to the council for a council burial. There was no way I was paying. I explained to the council that I wanted nothing to do with it and told them where they could find his documents. He had told me consistently over the years that they were under the unit in the lounge in a small brown box with his will, life insurance and everything else important. The council informed me that they had done a home check and couldn't find anything. The situation was very confusing. I said that I'd go over there and then sign everything over once I had had a look for the documents and removed anything that was mine or that I wanted. I took Joanna with me. I expected when I arrived that I would feel something, remorse, guilt, anything. When we went into the flat, I didn't feel anything. I just felt indifferent. I felt happy in my old room where I had experienced many happy events, but the rest of the place, it wasn't my abode. It wasn't my home. I had no connection to it and suddenly, I didn't feel guilty for it at all. I said to myself again that is what he did to us. I wanted to find some photos and really that was it. Everything was as I had last left it. I could see that the council had been in as there were drawers pulled out and some piles of documents. They obviously hadn't found what they were looking for. The woman from downstairs told me that someone from the council had been round and taken some golf clubs and other things. I did inform her that nothing should have been touched until I signed it all over, but she knew very little. I did twig that it must have been his friend. The person he treated more like a son than his own child. That didn't bother me though. I could only assume that Trevor had received the letter and decided he didn't like what it said. The truth.

I was annoyed that he had gotten rid of his will and insurance. Not that I wanted to make any money, but at least if it covered funeral costs or something, that would have been good. That was Trevor's final two fingers up to me. He must have got the letter and thought, 'fuck you'. I expect that he assumed I would be left to foot the bill of his funeral and that would be his legacy to me, leaving me stone broke. Sorry Trevor, not on my watch. There was no remorse in him and that ensured that I felt totally justified in my actions. Trevor was dead, there was no longer any sensation of fear or anxiety. I had no need to feel bad or let down or pressured. I had no worries anymore. No fears. The freedom was there for me to take. Joanna and I searched the flat for anything of value and came across mostly porn. I took the TV and a ring. That was it. A big thankyou to my dad for everything he had never done and then leaving me with all his rubbish. He had his lifetime of rubbish and I just didn't want to sift through it all. I just left it. I had no use for any of it. I had no respect for the person to sort it and have it removed. I signed on the dotted line with the council. I walked down the stairs thinking about Sasha, Sabre, Squeak, Snoop and the last dog he had, Kane. I thought of all the times I had laughed with my friends there. Loved there. All the good memories of my life. I looked back up the stairs as I reached the bottom and said goodbye. Then I locked the door on the flat in

Vorfield Close, walked to the car and I never went back. Never looked back. All those years I had spent stressing, in depression, all it took was for my father to pass away and it was like the shackles had been taken off my feet. Freedom felt incredible.

As the funeral approached, I got messages from Trevor's friends calling me all sorts of terrible names. I just replied and said to them all that if they wanted a copy of the letter, then they were welcome to know what Trevor was really like. At that stage, I would have sent the letter to anyone who dared to tell me what a lovely man he was. They knew nothing. They, like everyone else, had been manipulated. He had received his karma. There was nothing I had to do. Trevor had been left by me. The one person he had left. I was the person that also hated him most. For all he did to me. I suddenly realised that I lingered around, almost driving myself mad, so that I could see him age, wither and when he got to his lowest ebb, I told him everything he had done to me and I walked out of there with my head held high. Him dying alone with no family or anyone there, was his karma. I never truly believed it would happen, but there it was in full, real life. I didn't hate anymore. I knew that deep down I had to forgive him and move on, because it was now my life. I had complete control and I was healing

I also wrote to Alison, but did I expect a response? When you have investigated the face of pure evil and survived, when you confront it, it will quiver at your strength. Alison was the monster. Her silence was a guilty plea. That was all I needed. It wasn't until I had grown and learnt more about these people, that I finally understood. Alison hated me and my sister, because we were in the way of her getting to our father. She wanted us out of the way, so she could get her claws into him. She had a daughter of her own who had epilepsy and had lots of seizures. I was confident in the thought that she took her rage out on myself and Laura, because we were normal, functioning children. I knew that Alison would have to live with that every day and the thoughts of what she had done to me and my sister. That was her fate. To live without Trevor in her life and to live with the terrible things she had done to us as children, was justification enough. She would also be truly alone. I felt it. I knew it. Never in a million years did I think I would feel so light and free. Trevor was gone. I couldn't explain the sense of release. It was like when a song captures your soul and you feel transcendent.

My mum also got a letter, and do you know what, it healed our relationship. I gave her a much more watered-down version of events, as I didn't want to cause her anymore pain. I understood why she left us. I understood everything my father did to her. There was no need to be at loggerheads or not talk. We were Trevor's victims. It should have, and it did make us all stronger together, not obliterate all of us into a thousand pieces. I knew my grandad and my nan would be smiling down on all of us. My grandad got his dying wish that we all made it back together as a family. That was also part of Trevor's misfortune. The family he had spent so many years separating, were now as strong as glue. United.

I was getting more confident and doing all the things I had always wanted to do. I even drove to Birmingham to see a concert on my own. I'd never have done that a few years before. I wasn't that frightened little boy anymore. For someone looking in on this world, you could see that I was deeply affected by everything that had happened to me, but I was still there, still breathing, still alive and still full of hope. That is one thing that would never, ever change. There were so many opportunities for me. If I wanted to, then all I had to do was to sit under the raging blue skies and take my pick. I could look over everything that had happened in my life without a sense of pain, loss or sorrow. It was a story. The imprints that had been made and the feelings of how I had let so much time slip away. How I'd spent so much time escaping. Getting wasted. Wasted time. The only regret I had was that I had let so much time slip away. At first, I thought all that time was barren and uncultivated but, it was time spent healing. That was never a waste. I see it now as that was me taking my time to come to terms with events. Working it out slowly. It obviously took me years to get over all of the happenings. I was about 11 years old when the abuse ended, and here I was 22 years later, finally getting over the fear. That paralysing agonising fear. I thought of all the things that had happened to me in my short but chaotic life, and came to realise that I was everything I had always been fated to be. Everything that had happened had led me to these decisions. I thought back to the year 2000, when we did the Ouija board in James's attic. "Send the letter". That was the letter. The letter that would set me free. Of course. The letter. That letter. That guidance. I never knew until that moment what it meant, but I felt that chill up my spine. It was truth. My great-grandad had told me all those years ago to send a letter. He must have been preparing me, setting me up, so the healing process could begin. He must have known it would take a long time for me to get back to myself. By saying it repeatedly, the words stuck firmly in my head when he repeated, "Send the letter.". It all made sense.

I remembered the evening so vividly in my mind. All those years it must have taken for me to build my strength and heal from the childhood abuse, and years for me to recover to a level where I could tell my father what he had done to me and begin to tell others. An age where I could stand up and make them accountable for their actions. That was when I knew I was truly healed. I wanted to share with people who may have been through the same things. Maybe then people would understand why my family is the way it is. Why we are the way we are. What Trevor and Alison had done not just to me, but to all of us. And for us to all finally move on. I felt that for years I must have had some form of Stockholm Syndrome or something, I just couldn't escape. I wasn't mentally strong enough to leave and go it alone. Then one day in that October of 2016, I suddenly realised that I was strong. I had put up with the years of abuse and the situation for so long. However, I had grown, I had surpassed all the hurt, pain, the blame and all the denying. I was the one. It was like an epiphany. I knew it was only me who could save myself. He was gone. I was with my mother, sister and family again. We had lost people on the way. My nan, grandad, and my uncle Steve, but we were still standing, the few who remained. I loved them all so much. I sometimes questioned if I felt nothing when Trevor died because I was so hardened and cold. These were thoughts that my anxiety constantly made me run through over and over and over and over. I brushed that thought away when I remembered how it felt especially at my nan's funeral, and I realised that I felt deeply. It was just because of the beatings and abuse and constant fear of Trevor, I had never developed any respect for him. But it was time to let go.

I let go of all the pain. I let it blow into the wind like a handful of white feathers. The rage and the bitterness ebbed away, because even though I couldn't find it, sometimes, I was still full of love and feeling. The feathers and memories floated off into the air and spread out, floating higher and higher, further and further apart, until they disappeared from sight. All the times I thought I was cold and empty and warped, it was still there, just hiding beneath the surface waiting to come out and be born again. Waiting for the tiny ember to reignite in my heart and mind and just love, be content and above all, free. The one thing I never thought would happen to me was to gain my freedom. Freedom from the terrible past, the thoughts, the drama and all the anxiety. I just let it all melt away. It was just like all the bruises from my childhood, the scar tissue and all the abuse, faded. The bruises faded. I could still feel them there, but they had gone to the extent where I was so genuinely happy with how far I'd come. I know I should have been a lot more grateful. Now I try to be a little bit better every day. It's a very long road. The psychic awareness or whatever it was, I learned it was all a part of me and to let it rule my life, would only end one way. The bad way, and it was time to stop living like that, get a grip and embrace it. I read about protecting myself and opening myself up to things, and I would sense more people and have more visitations. Nothing that I didn't feel uncomfortable with. I knew I could feel things. I had always had a feeling that if I met anyone or spoke to a medium that they would say something. Deep down, I knew what they would say. I felt it in my bones. I'd just never been, because I didn't want someone to confirm my thoughts. We had seen people on ghost nights and they had been attracted to me and what we got to happen, but I'd never really taken it too much further. All the heartache and the desperate times now gone, I couldn't stop pinching myself that it was over.

2018 – Inner Dream

Rounding a corner, I came into a room. I thought how odd that was, as I was sure I had just been in the bath. A curious feeling and haze swept over me. There was a single candle in the centre of the room. It glowed in the blackness. Oddly. I didn't think to turn on the light, I just kept looking at the flame, bobbing gently up and down. I saw something change in the darkness. It was as if the darkness moved. Fast. I grabbed out and felt a texture that was soft, but invisible. The shadows danced in the darkness around me, swirling high and fast. The room suddenly began to extend and I felt like my legs were on a conveyor belt. I began to move forward. The room appeared to turn into a corridor that extended out ahead of me. There were suddenly bright lights on the ceiling that were blinding. It took a few seconds of confusion before I realised that the walls were moving. They were getting closer together. They were moving inward. I felt the pangs of anxiety suddenly set in. I hadn't felt that feeling for a long time. My inner voice said, "Run. Run now!". I had to survive. Instinct kicked in and I ran. It was an unearthly run as I was moving at an unhuman speed. I wanted to get out quickly before the walls moved in on me, but they continued to move faster. Quicker. Closer. The walls moved closer and closer together, as I ran faster and faster. I could feel my heart beating through my chest. The intensity in the need to get to that door at the end before the walls closed in completely, was extreme. It wouldn't be long before they were killing me, squashing me flat, like a bug. Sweat collected on my face and ran down my nose, dripping, soaking my clothes as I tried to run. Faster and faster. It was as if I was moving as fast as an electrical current in a small wire, but the wire was closing in so quickly.

Above my head, the lights began to crack, split and go out as the walls crushed them in. Shards of glass rained down on me, sticking into my head, arms, legs and every uncovered piece of skin. Thousands of tiny cuts, opening up and spilling blood. There was no time to think about this as I continued to run. Anticipation building, the heart ready to explode and lungs burning. I looked down, head forward as I aimed for the goal. Darkness ensuing. Suddenly I fell to my knees down a step, through the door. Thank God, I had made it. I stood there, panting in the blackness. A faint light on either side of me drew my eyes, tiny sparks. I thought this was very strange and then, "wham", the walls came together. All my bones crunched. Every single part of my matter was pulverised, fatally flattened between the walls. I sat up in bed. A dream... well, a nightmare. I could still feel where my bones had broken and shattered. A deep, soul burning pain. The smarting faded as quickly as it came though. I still had the occasional nightmare. I often wondered if they were memory dreams of the past or if they were just general anxiety dreams, who could say. All I knew was that since my father had passed away, the dreams had lessened and I had very little anxiety, unless it was regarding something new that I was doing. I knew the dreams would fade away in time as my intuition grew and my mind expanded.

I went downstairs to look at things that I had gathered, some memories from Trevor's flat, including photos that belonged to his grandmother on that side and I put together a timeline. I didn't have anyone to help me. I searched through all the photographs and birth certificates and death certificates, I put the pieces together all by myself. It was like my ancestors wanted me to have a cohesive history. Although I knew nothing about my grandparents on my dad's side and my great grandparents, I had pictures and other mementos, so it was like I knew them. I was never alone. I found a book in Falmouth town with a photo of my dad in the London marches in the 1980's with the mining crew. I was free of any negativity towards Trevor now. It was over. I had forgiven him a long time ago, more for his sake than mine. But I'd never forget. Never ever. I could take that memory and put it into part of my history, where I came from. The experiences that had made me, me. Being comfortable with who I was, where I had come from, what I had been through. I had a future to look forward to.

I knew I was on the right track. Every time I felt a tingle up my spine or when I would suddenly sense that my nan was there. I assume it was my nan anyway. I let go of all the past. It was in June of 2018 that I went to finally visit a medium. It was very strange as she asked me if she had read me before. I said no. She replied that, "this would be very interesting." She spoke of my nan and great-grandad and told me a few things. This blonde lady with a lot of wisdom said to me that I had a warrior woman with me. She was my spirit guide and she held a crossbow. I found that odd but believable, as thirty minutes before I had told Joanna that I wanted a Buffy toy with a crossbow. She even said that Trevor came through and could see everything from my point of view and he was sorry. He knew that I had been right. I felt that even if it wasn't real, then it was still some further closure. She also said to me exactly what I thought she would say. That I could do exactly what she does. She said I am so open that I just do things without even trying. I would think of things to ask her and suddenly, she would start talking about them. When I said that to her, she said I was reading her. She spoke of a shadow figure. It twigged in my mind from all those years ago. She said that it was seeking help for what I could do. She thought I had a strength in moving things, spirits energy on. I immediately thought of the black dog and the incident at the man's flat and the overdose. They had moved on when they got acknowledgement. Whatever the shadow person had been, it must have known what I could do back then, long before I knew I could do it and it was reaching out to me for help. I just didn't understand and was terrified. I got the chill up my spine as I wrote that, as it felt right. I left feeling elated.

I spent the next few months sort of living my childhood again. It was like I was released and growing. Re-growing and recharging. Enjoying things I should have been back then when I was so shut off and seeking any sort of comfort and guidance. So, I listened to all the music I grew up with. There had been an announcement that the Spice Girls were getting back together. I waited for the tickets to be released and I bloody well got them. I was going to see the Spice Girls! My childhood dream was coming true. I was learning guitar like I had always wanted to do. All Saints and Aqua were also back. It was like a nostalgia fest. I was experiencing things I had only dreamt of, in terms of seeing my idols perform. I had a steady life. I worked. I saw my family. I spent time doing things I loved. I knew I wanted to write this book, so that I could connect with the child I used to be. To go through as much of the pain as I could remember and write it down. Stick it in a box. This being the box, and then moving on. Kind of a therapy.

It started out as something totally different and I've been doing it for maybe 14 years, but it evolved into what it is. I can only explain that's how I feel right now, that this is the right way to write things. I wanted to preserve names and places at first, but thought why should I hide? I can do the things I please. I have no-one to hold me back now. I don't regret a thing as it has all brought me to where I am today. I can say I made it. I survived. If I could send a message back to myself in time, I would say to myself to be brave and be strong, as it does get better. It did get better. I got into my car, a silver Toyota Rav 4. My trusty steed that had got me through floods, snow and countless good times. I drove from home, past Tehidy woods, to the top of the cliffs. The sun rays crept over the horizon as the sun began to rise. There was a heavenly glow, orange and bright. The landscape was beautiful and enchanting as it stretched out before me. The waves crashed on a choppy sea below. A turquoise green, deep and clear. I felt no fear. No angst. Just free. Peace. Blessed with this new sense of knowledge and life, I moved on. Drove away, all day, smiling. Music playing as I approached a new road, somewhere untravelled.

I had a dream last night about being back in Plain-an-Gwarry. It had all been freshly renovated and I was looking around it with the intentions of trying to move in. It was airy and light. Roomy. I felt at ease there and there was nothing negative about it at all. I wanted to be there and looked around with expectancy. That is some sort of healing as that is where I remember most of my growing and fear. I also dreamt about a hazy sun filled time when Trevor and I played. I remember in the dream thinking to myself that there were some very happy moments in between everything else. That was when I knew I was really getting over everything. I was reaching a place where I had processed everything. 35 years old and I was now able to start being who I should have been a long time ago. The obsessive behaviours I had, were falling away. I cleaned a lot less. I got a lot less stressed. I slept better. I even gave up the cigarettes, which was one of the best things I ever did. If I even have a drag now, I feel ill. I began to exercise. The negative self-destructive behaviours shrunk away. Even playing the guitar was something I wanted, but never imagined I'd be able to do. I learnt on the guitar Richie got me that I'd kept all that time, I always kept pieces of things and people that had been important to me. They say time heals. It does. It will. It has. I used to think that there wasn't any time. But there is. I look back and think that there really is time for everything. There is so much time.

2019 - Spice mania

So, 20 years after my first ever obsession began, I would finally be going to see the Spice Girls. To some, they may think it's funny or a joke. They may snigger or laugh or say, "Why would you want to go and see them?", but it was my choice. It was my dream. I had been waiting for the moment for years and years. As I stood there in the crowd of thousands of people, I felt myself revert to how I felt at 12 years old. How they made me feel back then. I felt like Geri singing, "Back where I belong now, was it just a dream", was a callout to me. All of a sudden, I realized I was exactly where I was meant to be, where I belonged. Then when 'Goodbye' rung out across the stadium, I realized it was time to say goodbye to that 12 year old version of me. That version of me that was destroyed and broken. The sides of me that had been traumatized and abused. That hopeful boy that didn't see a real way out. He had made it, that was me. I was 11 when the abuse had ended. I was healing from then and who knew I would spend the next 20 plus years healing. As I reconnected with that boy from all those years ago, all the old feelings came back. However, they had changed. I didn't feel that crippling fear anymore. It was almost like it had happened to someone else. As I saw my childhood idols in the flesh, I was saying goodbye to that child. The one that lived in the fear, the pain, the crippling agony. Heavy loneliness I had carried for so long. "Goodbye my friend. I know you're gone you said you're gone, but I can still feel you here…".

I won't ever let myself go, as that little boy is still me. But I reached a point in my life where I had dealt with all the negativity. I had got over it and that was it now. I had put in a box and put it away. There was no need to hold on to it anymore. I can't even describe how it makes me feel inside. I used to feel the emptiness. Now I feel a fulfilment that means I got through it. It may have taken me years and years from the 5 year old boy to the 35 year old man I grew into. I made it. And I did it with the help of these girls. The music. It all made me feel elated, teary-eyed with righteousness and happiness. A sense of nostalgia and peace. I cannot put the feelings into words. It really was a dream for so long. And dreams come true; I felt for a moment that I was that 12 year old boy again. Not the one who was terrified, alone and in pieces. But the tiny small part of that 12 year old me that was strong and defiant and would carry on. That part of me that was like, "Come on!" whenever I played the Spice Girls and got lost in the music. That version of me that somewhere deep down knew I would make it one day. That small tiny part of me that would learn to grow in the world and become stronger than anyone else. We all handle our pain differently and some people may deal with mine easier than I did. Others would crumble. But like the tour with the Spice Girls in my 35th year, that was my journey. I had come full circle. I didn't need merchandise and items to fill my life anymore. I had the greatest memory that I had been dreaming of for most of my life. When a dream comes true, it makes you think that all the struggles, ups and downs, the deep lows do come through. The little, terrified boy was laid to rest and I thanked my idols for seeing him through those times. While I remember everything, and I thought it would never end, its like a whole other life.

You can still be there all those years later and still achieve something you really wanted. To some it may be so little, but for me, it was everything. Absolutely everything. They wrote some songs that I connected with in a way like no other before. I had just started to overcome horrific abuse and was regaining some sense of control in my life. I was hitting puberty and hormones were kicking in. I didn't know who I was or what I was. Then these five girls came along with a powerful message that you could be whoever you wanted to be. It didn't matter who you were. Everyone was part of the gang. I connected with music in a new and totally different way. Sometimes it was an escape. This was a pure joy. They took me away from everything in my own life. The crippling loneliness, all the pain and hurt that I bottled deep down inside. They had a certain power and people were drawn to it. I always sat at home looking through my scrapbooks, magazines and the posters and dreamt that one day I would see my idols live. At that age I didn't really know the full effect that live music can have on your soul. I learnt this as I grew older. Fans were frenzied for these girls. It was like being in a huge unspoken family. I never really met anyone who loved them on the level I did, but you never know. I could live in hope. These five girls took me to a place where I was free of my doubts and free of any of my anguish. There was no hate, just pure love. Even then I don't think they knew the effect they had on me and so many other people all over the world. To see 40,000 people all singing the same songs together, meant everything to me. It was an absolute dream come true. I was overwhelmed with joy. I had truly spiced up my life!

Now

The Corrs, "Forgiven, not Forgotten" played quietly on the car radio. In the end, I did learn to forgive. But I never would forget. I knew that I had to let go of the feelings of what my father had done to me. I took my lead from an episode of Buffy. I was influenced by Buffy and still am to this very day. There is an episode where Giles tells her that you don't forgive to suit yourself. You forgive because the other person needs, it regardless of what you think. To forgive is an act of mercy, compassion. My compassion freed me and ensured I was not like Trevor. I never would be.

Sitting thoughtfully in the bright sunlight on the water's edge, I breathed deeply. The road ahead was unknown, but there was a certainty within me. I had some sort of new strength and I was revitalised. I knew that nothing would ever be the same again and I was free to do anything I wanted, be whatever I wanted to be. My life was my own. As limited as it had been, it was mine and no-one else's – I was grateful for that. The sun began to sink beneath the horizon, and I pulled myself to my feet, such strong sturdy feet that would hold up the weight of the world now and forever more. Walking into the sunset, this brilliant adaptation of me watched as the yellows and oranges darkened to reds, before they eventually sunk into the sea, extinguished by the waves, then gone. I knew that even though it was dark now, the sun would rise again. It was the only guaranteed thing, the sun comes up, goes down and then comes up again. It would continue when I was long gone, dead and buried with the ancestors I now missed, returning to the sands of time where they first came from. I had gone head to head, eye to eye with the devil and won. I wanted to wait for the sun to rise again, but knew I would soon tire and fall asleep. I wanted to see the first rays, like fingers of hope rising in the sky, but I knew there would be many, many days yet where I could do this. I returned home. I looked up at my nan and grandad's cuckoo clock that now resided in my hallway and smiled with the memory of them. I looked from the window at the bright moon in the sky. Everything was quiet. For the first time in a long time, everything was just silent and peaceful. The moon glowing like an emperor with his crown shining bright and effervescent. Time had passed, hurt had happened, but I had won. It was not a battle I had chosen at all, but I had survived and was there to relive the tale, recount the extraordinary journey and dream sweet, pleasant dreams. Knowing that when I woke, it would be the first day of my new life. My life. The future looked brighter than it had ever done. I prayed for sweet dreams.

Chapter 10

Facing a monster

I saw a request on Facebook for information regarding The Old Dairy in Plain and Gwarry, so I eagerly messaged the man and told him I had lived there some years before. He told me no one had lived there since I had moved out, not for very long anyway, and invited me over to come and look at the old place. To be honest, I was terrified, but I was drawn to go and revisit the scene of so much good, and bad.

I parked at the top of the lane. As I approached the house, I imagined all the old feelings of foreboding might return. They didn't. As I entered the house, I saw the old wood panelling downstairs, the thick flat bannister at the bottom of the stairs. The bathroom was the same as it had been all those years before. The lounge was half ripped out and being rearranged. A million memories flashed in my mind, but I took control of them and held them close. As I scaled the stairs, I ran my fingers up the wall to my right and up the bannister on the left. The same holes in the walls were there, where Trevor had hung his dog pictures. I entered my old bedroom. The dark caverns where the locks had been attached were still there. The slope that held my bed. The cracks in the paint were all still present, even after so much time. I recalled every detail. I traced the cracks with my fingers. I didn't feel sad, upset or angry. My memory delved into every moment. Every laugh, every tear. In a weird way, because I had made peace with everything, it felt like it was mine. My place. Nearly every aspect of the house, identical to when we had moved out. The sick and sinking feeling had long since dissipated. I left with a sense of freedom and peace in my heart and mind. I felt like I had returned home, even though I was convinced it would be a monstrous revisit. I had needed to return at that moment as part of my healing process. I could have moved back in that very day if it had been offered. Somehow, I had come home, but only for the good memories. The rest had slipped away with the sands of time.

Something miraculous can happen to you when you feel inspired and you feel healed. There was an event that I never thought would happen. On some level, I wanted it to happen. I had dreamt about all the ways it could have happened and could have potentially played out. I never in my wildest imaginings thought it would happen though. As the winter solstice of 2019 approached, I knew it was time to make the final clearance of everything that had plagued me for so long. Empty myself of every last bit of emotion I had for those two abusers. I had always wanted to confront my abusers, but never thought I would be able to or be able to get any sort of closure for it. My father passed away without a hint of remorse. I often wondered if Alison would go the same way. Throughout my life I had learnt the monsters were real. I could cope with everything else except the fear that sprang from those two people.

As 2019 drew to a close, I thought I had done everything I had to do on the trajectory I was on, it had been years since I'd started the healing process and confronted everything I had to. I had returned to Plain-an-Gwarry. I had revisited my past. I suddenly came to realize I had one thing left to do. I knew what it was.

1, 2, 3, 4. The numbers had been appearing to me for such a long time. I would see them everywhere. I saw them the day before. I saw them through the years. Like a message through time. Like the letter I had been prepared to send many years ago, I always felt that 1, 2, 3, 4 was a message, but I didn't understand its meaning. I had had a fantastic year. I had a sudden intrusive thought that I wanted to try and contact Alison one last time to see if she would speak to me. I didn't expect much. I didn't even know if she would answer the phone or engage with me. I tried to google her name for a number or an address. It was only when I asked my nan for some help and low and behold, I found the number within five minutes. I just wanted her to know before she passed away like Trevor, that I was still here and that I hadn't forgotten. I thought I had better try to phone it, so I withheld my number. Three rings and she answered. I dropped the phone down immediately. I felt that twang of fear. It had been a long time since I had felt that. It wasn't an unfamiliar feeling, but it had lessened. This was it. I was going to do this. I felt like I needed a final moment. A final push to change my life, my story, my way. I knew that this was what I wanted to do. I asked my friends for advice about if I should phone her back and speak to her. I was worried she would want full control over me and just hang up. Maybe I thought she would be a complete bitch and say awful things down the phone to me. I wondered if she would be that nasty that she would think she still held power over me. I felt deep inside that whatever the outcome, that that wasn't the case. Whatever happened during this phone call, I was strong. I was there at that stage in my life preparing to confront my demon. Either way, I remembered what I had learnt from Buffy and asked myself the question; are you ready to be strong? I knew that this was the final part of whatever healing or task I was to do. Deep down I felt this was the right time. The right path. I was meant to get to this point.

I dialed the number again. The line began to ring. "Hello", answered Alison. My mind began to swirl. I felt the same old fear that I had felt as a child. I was about to go head to head with my demon. The original monster that had scared me in the dark. The voice echoing in the silence, laughing at my misfortune.

"Hello, is that Alison?", I stammered. "Yes, who is that?", she enquired. I wasn't sure if she already knew who it was or if she genuinely didn't know. The feeling I got was that she was not expecting to hear from me. Clearly, she had always thought she had got away scot free with no consequence to her actions.

"It's Andrew."

"Who?", she asked.

"Andrew Turvill".

"Oh, right, yes", she replied. I felt like my tongue was tied, but I immediately said that I would like to have an adult discussion and that I wanted some closure. I asked her if she had heard about what had happened with Trevor. She merely said, "yes". She didn't answer any further than that. I guess that I had so much to say that she wouldn't have gotten a word in edgeways anyway. She hadn't hung the phone up. My heart was beating fast.

How many people confront their abusers? How many people work up the strength and the courage to do that. I never felt particularly brave in life. However, this was the bravest thing I think I had ever done. I didn't realize how brave I was until that moment. The amalgamation of all the events that had led me to that moment, all the times I had felt that fear, hidden under my covers, been afraid to go home, every one of those moments. Every time I thought I had reached the point I was meant to, there was another. I mean when I felt guided through life to deal with events. I had spent the last few years healing and getting over everything. I truly thought I had done everything I had to do. Until that day, that moment, that phone call. This time I felt that this was the final one. The final hurdle to my emotional freedom I hadn't foreseen it or even expected it to happen, it just was, and for that I knew it was the true end. "I don't want to make a list of everything that happened", I said as I composed myself, trying to not let my voice tremble or show any sign of weakness. "We both know what happened, obviously". I continued to say. I began to stumble over my words and stutter. She made no attempt to butt in, I assumed she was still on the line. "I just want to know that nothing was ever mine and my sisters' fault that went on.". She agreed with a, hmm-mm, and let me continue.

When I asked her if she knew what had happened to my father, she said she didn't, so I went into full depth. I told her that the way I left him alone at the end was payback for how he had treated me. What they had done to me. Her replies were very short and I could tell from her voice that she was slowly breaking. Something had changed in her, was it age? Was it remorse? I didn't know. I just wanted to say my piece.

I explained to her about how I had written him a letter before he passed away and asked her if she knew anything about that. She said she had no knowledge of it at all so I continued. "I want to know if you can acknowledge what happened and just say that there is remorse somewhere?". "Yes, yes there is", she stuttered. I could feel and hear her voice breaking. As I explained more about Trevor and those final days, I heard her heart sink. As an empath, I felt it. That's how I knew she was remorseful. I almost felt as if I should feel sorry for her. Maybe it was just disappointment and pity.

"That's good", I said, "It's been 25 years since he last hit me, and it has taken me this long to get back to who I should be. Trevor passing away was the key that freed me".

"Yes, I understand that", she replied. There was a lot of agreeance sounds. I didn't really have time to process what she was saying. The sounds and the feelings were in the right place and the thought never crossed my mind that it could just be another act of this monster. I knew it was genuine. I just knew it. I just know that she was not expecting to hear from me. She probably never expected for me to stand up, speak out and make her accountable for her own actions. The two of us could not hide any of the events that had happened, because I remembered everything. Between the two of us, just us two, no-one else, she could not hide. She knew everything and she knew that I knew. There was nowhere to conceal herself. There was no denying. She didn't have to give me full sentences of explanations as we both knew the details. All I wanted was acknowledgement and acceptance of what she and he did.

I told her that I didn't want to go into individual events, but that I remembered everything. Every last abuse. Every detail. I knew she understood this. I didn't have to use the actual words. I told her that even he didn't know the full extent of everything and mentioned the holiday at the chalet. Her voice dropped further. I didn't want to say she sexually abused me. I didn't have to. She knew.

My mind was awash with all the questions I had always wanted to ask and all the things I wanted to say. Everything I had planned to get off my chest for years and years. "Him dying meant I don't have to be afraid anymore", I felt my voice quiver. I was holding strong. I recounted how angry I had been at Trevor leaving everything for me to pay for by removing his will and life insurance. I could hear the disgust in her response. "He knew what was going on, because he was part of it", I said shakily. "When we would sit downstairs and you would say I'd stuck my fingers up at you and he would agree". I heard her recall the events and her voice also shook. There was something there. There were the tones I had somehow dreamt of hearing. Some remorse. Some thought that she had done severely wrong by me and my family. Some glimmer of humanity. It almost removed all my bottled rage because this evil monster now had a human like quality. Maybe it was age. Maybe it was time. Maybe she had lost people important to her and had realized what she had done. To me it felt like she hadn't really thought about the events until I confronted her. For me, I had lived with those events playing like movies over and over in my mind continuously for years. That is what they had done to me.

"Laura said I used to have to sit on my hands to make sure one of you didn't say I'd stuck my fingers up". I was on the edge of crying as I actually spoke aloud details of the abuse to the actual abuser. She did not disagree with one single thing though. I could tell from the tone of her voice she was sick to the stomach. I could feel that ache of guilt in the pit of her belly that would eat at her from now on. I knew she would carry everything with her until the end of her days.

In a weird way it felt as if everything I had been carrying, that had weighed me down for years was, gone. I had passed it onto her. It had returned to the person who gave some of it out. It was her burden to bear now. Deep down I knew she wasn't as strong as me. She never would be. 25 years echoed around my mind. 25 years just to heal. Maybe only start to heal. I recounted how I was made to stand in the corner and write lines for hours and hours. "We never did anything wrong, did we?" I asked her, I wasn't breaking down, but I knew I was slowing, releasing some tears as I went.

"No, no, you didn't", she croaked, her voice low and sorrowful. I was taking no pleasure from it at all. I didn't really feel anything. In that moment, I was running on pure bravery.

"You made out that we did things wrong and made us feel wrong, when deep down we always knew it wasn't us". "Hmmm", she squeaked out.

"I could have grown up so differently", I said, "if he hadn't beaten me within an inch of my life and broken me down. I could have been so much more, done better in life. He controlled all of us.".

I asked her what was going on. She agreed with me that we were pawns to get at my mum. I told her that I could have been in a much better job or tried a bit harder in life and that Laura would have also been better. She agreed with every single word. Every syllable. She felt terrible. When I asked her if she had gone to the funeral, she said no. I don't really know what that meant, but I wondered if she had tried to get away from him as well. I didn't really care. This was about me. My moment. My face to face. Well, voice to voice, but that was enough. I had no simmering anger left. I had not one speck of hatred for this woman. The baton was passed. I had expected her to be spiteful and blame me and Laura for everything. Instead, I was confronting a person who was broken by what they had done. She sounded sad and pathetic. When confronted with every little nasty thing she had done, she could not deny it. I mean how could she deny it to me? It confirmed that everything that had happened to me had happened. I didn't dream it. I didn't imagine it. All the times that I thought maybe I'm crazy and had just created all these elaborate lies because I was somehow mentally ill. It was all real. None of it was made up.

I explained how I went back to Plain-an-Gwarry and how it made me feel. How I'd closed that door. Her voice was lighter at this, as if she had felt better that I was getting better. I thought this is the moment. I turned the knife. I said, "I even remember you pouring water or whatever it was on me in my bed when I was little.".

The only noise she made was a high pitched agreeing, hmm-mm sound. I could tell that was almost her breaking point. As she remembered what she had done to me some 30 years ago, she almost showed me more emotion than I had ever seen or heard from her. I felt that. She was either crying on the end of the phone or about to. At that moment I think she truly felt how I felt and realized the full extent of what she had done. I also believe that she was shocked that I remembered such detail. She could not escape. The tables had turned and it was as if I were the bigger person now and she was the frightened one who could not escape.

I sensed I was releasing all these little parts of me that I had held onto for so long. I felt so good. What I think was better was that I was releasing them to the actual person who created them and gave them to me in the first place. I was returning them to their sender. What a wild experience this was. I felt sort of euphoric and terrified and brilliant all at the same time. I felt justified in everything I had ever done. Every little positive step I had made by myself on the long road to healing. It was all down to me. Everything I had done up until that moment had led me there. Trevor had died without ever showing me this kind of emotion. He had shown nothing. "I just always wanted to ask to you, why? Why would you do that? If you had never done any of that, he would never have started to beat us". I heard her sniff. There were obviously tears. I didn't think that would be a question she could answer, because she probably didn't even know why herself. She did say he would have probably been brutal towards me and Laura anyway, as that was his type of personality. And I explained that she had exacerbated it for sure. Someone must have come home or walked into the room at her end, as she suddenly said, "I am sorry, but I have to go". I had said everything I wanted to say except one thing. "You will not her from me again, Alison. I just wanted to speak to you and tell you that I am strong. You did not break me. You came pretty close, but I am still here. It's taken me more than 25 years, but I am here. I survived.".

I left it at that and hung the phone up.

I looked down at the phone. I had called at 12.34 and the call had lasted 12 minutes and 34 seconds. My mind swirled. 1,2,3,4. That was the time I had rung her. This was the message. I had been seeing this sequence numbers for years and years and years. That was the exact right moment in time for me to make contact with Alison. It was clearly always going to happen. Everything in my life had guided me to that moment to make that call at that time. I felt lighter. The weight had been lifted and I was free. I immediately messaged the medium Debbie I had seen to ask her and she replied with, "What a beautiful synchronicity and way for the universe to say, I got your back.".

I felt elated, I had gotten more from the short conversation with Alison than I realized. More than I expected and more than I knew I needed. I couldn't condone anything she had done, but the fact that there was a hint of remorse, gave me the power. It made me self-assured that I was right and just. That she knew I remembered every detail even from being five years old. She had to live with that now. It was like a relay race and I had stuck out doing my part and now I had passed the baton onto her. She was the final person in the race and she had to carry it until the end from then on. My mind was light. My heavy shoulders were lifted. I was truly free. Truly at peace. So, I headed into the year 2020 free, it's the only way to be. How was I to know a pandemic was around the corner!? Just when things are going right, hey?

I end my story sitting happily, looking over my life listening to, "Hands clean" by Alanis Morrissette and "Someday" by Sugar Ray. "Some say, better things will come my way, some way, when the sun begins to shine. I hear a song from another time and fade away... and fade away.".

As I lay sleeping in my bed, I felt myself lucid dreaming. I heard birds chattering and sensed optimistic sunlight. I could feel my childhood self regenerating and growing in the light. The connections I had made with myself meant that I could truly lay everything to rest. Everything I had been through, fought and thought. I was healed. I had done it myself. I could feel the childish giggling brewing in me. I was running through fields, looking at the big red flowers, the ones that only grew in that one place in the whole world. I saw myself so young. I felt I was there to watch over him, me. All those years that would pass and somehow, subconsciously I was there looking after myself all along. I couldn't see anything after this because that burning ball in the sky, burnt so vividly. I heard myself and my sister playing and squealing, like when we were children in my nan's garden. My sister singing a tune. I tried to focus in the intense sunlight and see something, but couldn't. The birds chirped louder and I could hear my nan's budgie squawking excitedly as my nan called to Albie, the dog. I felt a child run by me and giggle. I heard my nan and granddad's cuckoo clock chime off in the distance, and heard an echoey voice faintly in the sunshine, birdsong and laughter. It was my grandad calling out, "Mary! He's been playing with that bloody cuckoo clock again!".

Some common signs that there may be something concerning happening in a child's life:

- o   unexplained changes in behaviours or personality
- o   becoming withdrawn
- o   seeming anxious
- o   becoming uncharacteristically aggressive
- o   lacks social skills and has few friends, if any
- o   poor bond or relationship with a parent
- o   knowledge of adult issues inappropriate for their age
- o   running away or going missing
- o   always choosing to wear clothes which cover their body.

Instagram @a_turvy